STORIES ABOUT SAINT JOHN PAUL II

Stories about
Saint John Paul II

told by his close friends and co-workers

Interviews with Wlodzimierz Redzioch

Translated from Italian and German by
Michael J. Miller

IGNATIUS PRESS   SAN FRANCISCO

Original Italian edition
Accanto a Giovanni Paolo II: Gli amici & I callaboratori raccontano
© 2014 by Edizioni Ares, Milan

Homily of His Holiness Benedict XVI
On the Occasion of the Beatification of the Servant of God John Paul II
© 2011 by Libreria Editrice Vaticana

This English-language edition has been realized by arrangement with Silvia Vassena

Cover design and photo by www.AmpersandMiami.com

"Spread in society,
without distinction as to race, class, culture or age,
the knowledge that we are all called to holiness.

Strive to be saints yourselves in the first place,
cultivating an evangelical style of humility and service,
of abandonment to Providence
and of constant listening to the voice of the Spirit.

In that way, you will be the 'salt of the earth'
and your light will 'shine before men,
that they may see your good works
and give glory to your Father who is in heaven'."

—*John Paul II*

CONTENTS

Wlodzimierz Redzioch
"He changed my life, too"   11

I. As the Pope Emeritus Remembers Him

His Holiness Benedict XVI
"It became increasingly clear to me that John Paul II
was a saint"   15

II. In the Pope's Apartment

Stanislaw Dziwisz
"From Kraków to Rome to the glory of the altars"   27

Emery Kabongo
"He was like the servant who went through the streets
inviting everyone to the King's banquet"   35

Mieczyslaw Mokrzycki
"He was convinced that he could offer mankind nothing
better than Jesus"   42

III. Longtime Friends

Andrzej Maria Deskur
"On his door they wrote: 'Future saint'"   53

Stanislaw Grygiel
"The pope who looked to the laity, the friend in whom
I recognized God's faithfulness"   59

Stanislaw Nagy
A close friendship that started in a train on the Kraków–
Lublin line   66

Wanda Póltawska
  Story of a spiritual friendship   72

IV. Co-workers in the Vatican

Joaquín Navarro Valls
  The "voice" of John Paul II   85

Pawel Ptasznik
  "His constant concern? The salvation of mankind"   93

Camillo Ruini
  "God made him his own. That is, he was a man of God"   99

Angelo Sodano
  "As though seeing him who is invisible"   106

V. Taking Care of the Pope

Egildo Biocca
  "On tour" with the pope   113

Renato Buzzonetti
  The heroic patience of the pope as a patient   119

Arturo Mari
  "I have photographed six popes. He considered me a son"   131

VI. Witnesses

Tarcisio Bertone
  "A guide, support, and example for everyone"   141

Javier Echevarría
  Sanctifying everyday life   148

Gianfranco Svidercoschi
  A pontificate that changed the Church   157

VII. Toward the Glory of the Altars

Angelo Amato
  "A saint, and so to be imitated"   167

Marie Simon Pierre Normand
  "John Paul II had the last word"   171

Floribeth Mora Díaz
  "A voice told me to get up from bed"   179

Slawomir Oder
  "I feel it is my duty to testify to the gifts I received
  as postulator"   185

VIII. Finally Blessed!

His Holiness Pope Benedict XVI
  Homily on the occasion of the beatification of John Paul II   195

IX. A Saint of Our Times

His Holiness Pope Francis I
  Homily on the occasion of the canonization of Blessed
  John XXIII and Blessed John Paul II   203

Acknowledgments   207

Note about the Author   209

Wlodzimierz Redzioch

"HE CHANGED MY LIFE TOO"

I was in Paris when Karol Wojtyła became pope. I was on Saint Peter's Square when Ali Agca tried to kill the pope who was changing the world. I lived close to John Paul II throughout his pontificate.

At the beginning, while it was extraordinary that a Pole should be seated on the Chair of Peter, I did not imagine the extent of Wojtyła's human and spiritual greatness. But as I stayed close to him and to his collaborators, at a certain point I realized he was a saint.

The more I discovered this fact, the less I spoke about it: it seemed to me like telling a secret. Now, though, that the Church, too, has acknowledged what so many of us have understood, I feel that I can tell, through the voices of his friends and co-workers, the story of Saint John Paul II.

After completing a degree in engineering at the Polytechnic Institute in Częstochowa and courses in African Studies at the University of Warsaw, I found myself in Paris: I was thinking about becoming a lay missionary in Africa.

Never would I have imagined that the election of the first Polish pope would change my life, too. The news of Karol Wojtyła's election as pope seemed to be an impossible dream, and yet it had happened. The son of "ever-faithful" Poland had ascended to the throne of Peter. Nor could anyone imagine that the pope would change the history of Poland, of the Church, and of the world.

After days of festivities, I returned to my normal routine of study and work, until two priest friends, Father Casimiro Przydatek, S.J., and Father Ksawery Sokolowski, were commissioned to organize a center for Polish pilgrims in Rome.

Father Sokolowski told me about the project and made a proposal of his own: "Why don't you come and help us? We need trained people who know the languages." And he added: "Don't forget that now the history of Poland is being made here."

I was still undecided: going to Rome would mean giving up my studies and a professional career and choosing an uncertain, unknown future. But even then the pope had made an impression on so many hearts, and on mine too, and after a few months of hesitating, I left the capital of France for that of Italy.

For years I accompanied the pilgrims who were being received in audience by John Paul II.

I spent more than thirty years in the offices of *L'Osservatore romano*, and I associated with many, many curial officials, prefects and presidents of dicasteries, archbishops and cardinals, co-workers of the last three pontiffs.

With this book I seek to make Karol Wojtyła better known—the man, the priest, and the pope—through stories told by people who served him, who were close to him, and who helped him to write the history of the Church and of the world.

In 27 years, John Paul II made 146 apostolic journeys in Italy and 104 abroad, visiting 129 countries: 822 days of traveling. In 147 beatification ceremonies, he proclaimed 1,338 Servants of God Blessed, and in 51 canonization ceremonies he proclaimed 482 saints. He wrote 14 encyclicals, 15 apostolic exhortations, 11 constitutions, 45 apostolic letters, in addition to annual messages for the World Day of Peace, the World Day of the Sick, World Youth Day, and the World Day of Social Communications.

In those twenty-seven years, the Polish pope changed the world: he did it, not by relying on sophisticated political strategies, but above all because he succeeded in touching and changing the hearts of people. True and lasting changes are not possible unless they are born in people's hearts.

In the book that you are about to read, the persons whom I interviewed tell about their encounter with Karol Wojtyła, in some cases even before he became pope, in joy and in suffering, in doubt and in certainty, in health and in sickness. You will discover many previously unpublished stories and anecdotes, and you will have the opportunity to know the great heart with which Karol Wojtyła loved God and mankind.

I

As the Pope Emeritus Remembers Him

His Holiness Benedict XVI

"IT BECAME INCREASINGLY CLEAR TO ME THAT JOHN PAUL II WAS A SAINT"

On the occasion of the canonization of John Paul II, the Holy Father Emeritus Benedict XVI, born Joseph Ratzinger, agreed to contribute to this volume by offering his personal remembrance of the saintly pope, his predecessor.

Your Holiness, the names of Karol Wojtyła and Joseph Ratzinger are connected, for different reasons, to the Second Vatican Council. Were you already acquainted during the council?

The first encounter between Cardinal Wojtyła and me that I am aware of took place only later, in the conclave in which John Paul I was elected.

During the council, we did both collaborate on the Constitution on the Church in the Modern World, but obviously on different sections, so we did not meet. In September 1978, when the Polish bishops visited Germany, I was in Ecuador as the personal representative of John Paul I. The Church of Munich and Freising is connected with the Ecuadorian Church by a "twinning" relationship established by Archbishop Echevarría Ruiz (Guayaquil) and Cardinal Döpfner. And so, very much to my regret, I missed the opportunity to meet the archbishop of Kraków personally. Naturally I had heard about his work as a philosopher and a pastor, and for some time I had wanted to become acquainted with him.

Wojtyła, for his part, had read my *Introduction to Christianity*, which he had even quoted during the spiritual exercises that he preached for Paul VI and the Curia during Lent of 1976. So it is as if interiorly we were waiting to meet each other.

From the start I had great esteem and a cordial sympathy for the metropolitan of Kraków. In the 1978 pre-conclave, he impressively analyzed for us the nature of Marxism. But above all, right away I felt strongly the human charm that emanated from him, and, from the way that he prayed, I sensed how profoundly united he was to God.

What did you feel when the Holy Father John Paul II called you to put you in charge of the Congregation for the Doctrine of the Faith?

John Paul II called me in 1979 to appoint me prefect of the Congregation for Catholic Education.

Only two years had passed since my episcopal consecration in Munich, and I thought it impossible to leave the See of Saint Corbinian so soon. After all, episcopal consecration was in some sense a promise of fidelity to my home diocese. I therefore asked the pope to refrain from making that appointment. He then called on Cardinal Baum of Washington for that position, but at that time announced that later on he would turn to me again with another commission.

It was probably sometime in 1980 that he told me that he intended to appoint me, in late 1981, prefect of the Congregation for the Doctrine of the Faith as the successor of Cardinal Šeper.

Since I continued to feel obliged with regard to my diocese, I took the liberty of setting a condition for my acceptance of the position, thinking that it was impossible to fulfill. I said that I felt the duty to continue publishing theological works. I would be able to say yes only if that was compatible with the job of prefect. The pope, who was always very kind and considerate to me, told me that he would become better informed about the question so as to form an opinion. During my next visit, he showed that theological publications are compatible with the office of prefect. Cardinal Garrone, too, he said, had published theological works as prefect of the Congregation for Catholic Education.

And so I accepted the commission, knowing the seriousness of the responsibility, but also conscious that obedience to the pope now required a Yes from me.

Could you tell us how the collaboration between you and John Paul II developed?

Collaboration with the Holy Father was always characterized by friendship and trust. It developed mainly on two levels: the official and the private.

Every Friday at 6:00 P.M., the pope receives in audience the prefect of the Congregation for the Doctrine of the Faith, who submits for his decision the problems that have come up. Of course doctrinal problems take precedence, and then there are also questions of a disciplinary nature—the laicization of priests who have requested it, granting the Pauline privilege for those marriages in which one of the spouses is non-Christian, and so forth. Later on, in addition, there was also the ongoing work on the *Catechism of the Catholic Church*.

In any case, the Holy Father received the essential documentation ahead of time and therefore was already familiar with the questions that would be discussed. In this way, we were always able to discuss theological problems together productively. The pope read very widely, in the latest German literature, too, and it was always nice—for both of us—to seek together the right decisions about all these matters.

Besides these actual official appointments, there were various types of semiofficial or nonofficial meetings.

I would call semiofficial the audiences in which for several years, every Tuesday morning, the Wednesday catecheses were discussed; membership in these groups varied.

By means of his catecheses, the pope had decided to offer a catechism over the course of time. He suggested the topics and had people prepare initial points for discussion. Since representatives of various disciplines were always present, these conversations were always very good and instructive; I like to recall them. Here, too, the theological competence of the pope was evident. At the same time, though, I admired his willingness to learn.

Finally, it was one of the pope's customs to invite to dinner the bishops who were making their *ad limina* visit, as well as other groups composed in various ways of bishops and priests, depending on the circumstance. These were almost always "working dinners" in which a theological topic was often proposed.

In the early days, there was a whole series of dinners in which the new Code [of Canon Law] was discussed bit by bit. It was a semi-final version that we worked through during those dinners, and in this way we prepared the final text. Later on, various topics were debated.

The large number of people present always made for a wide-ranging conversation. And yet there was always a place for good humor, too. The pope liked to laugh, and so these working dinners, for all the seriousness of the matter, were in fact occasions to be in cheerful company.

What were the doctrinal challenges that you faced together during your years at the Congregation for the Doctrine of the Faith?

The first major challenge that we faced was the theology of liberation that was spreading in Latin America. Both in Europe and in North America, it was generally thought that this was a way of helping the poor and therefore a cause that one could only approve on all sides. But that was an error.

Certainly poverty and the poor were addressed by liberation theology—from a very specific perspective, however. Programs of direct aid to the poor and reforms that improved their condition were condemned as "reformism" that has the effect of reinforcing the system: it was claimed that these methods appeased the rage and indignation that were necessary for the revolutionary transformation of the system. It was not a question of aid and reforms, they said, but of a major upheaval that could usher in a new world. The Christian faith was used as the engine for this revolutionary movement and was thus transformed into a political force. The religious traditions of the faith were placed at the service of political action. Thereby the faith was profoundly alienated from itself, and so also genuine love for the poor was neutralized.

Of course several variations of these ideas were current, and they were not always presented with absolute clarity, but overall that was the gist. It was necessary to oppose such a falsification of the Christian faith, precisely for sake of the poor and of the service performed for them.

On the basis of his experiences in his Polish homeland, John Paul II provided us with the essential clarifications. On the one hand, he had firsthand knowledge of the enslavement brought about by the

Marxist ideology that acted as the godfather of liberation theology. From his own painful experience, it was clear to him that it was necessary to resist this type of "liberation". On the other hand, precisely the situation in his homeland had shown him that the Church must truly work for freedom and liberation, not in a political way, but by awakening in men, through faith, the forces of genuine liberation. The pope directed us to speak about both these aspects: on the one hand, to unmask a false idea of liberation; on the other hand, to set forth the Church's genuine vocation to the liberation of man.

This is what we tried to say in the two instructions on liberation theology that stood at the beginning of my work in the Congregation for the Doctrine of the Faith.

One of the chief problems of our work, during the years when I was prefect, was the struggle to arrive at a correct understanding of ecumenism.

Here, too, it was a two-sided matter: on the one hand, the task of bringing about unity must be presented in all its urgency, and paths leading to it must be opened up; on the other hand, we must reject false views of unity, which would try to arrive at unity of faith by the shortcut of watering down the faith.

Documents on various aspects of ecumenism originated in this context. Among them, the one that provoked the strongest reactions was the declaration *Dominus Iesus* in 2000, which summarizes the indispensable elements of the Catholic faith.

The dialogue among world religions remains a central topic; however, we were able to publish only a few rather short documents on this theme.

We sought to address the question slowly and tentatively, above all through discussions with theologians and bishops' conferences. Especially important was the meeting in Hong Kong with the doctrinal commissions of the bishops' conferences of the Asian countries. The question will certainly continue to be one of the main challenges for a long time to come.

Another major challenge was our participation in the preparation of the Holy Father's encyclical *Veritatis splendor* on problems of moral theology.

Lastly, we dealt also with the question about the nature and task of theology in our time. To many people today, scholarly standards [*scientificità*] and ties with the Church seem to be to a great extent mutually contradictory. Nevertheless, theology can continue to exist solely in and with the Church. We published an instruction on this question.

Which of the many encyclicals of John Paul II do you consider the most important?

I think that there are three particularly important encyclicals. In the first place, I wish to mention *Redemptor hominis*, the pope's first encyclical, in which he presented his personal synthesis of the Christian faith.

This document is a sort of *summa* of his own struggle with the faith and thus presents a comprehensive view of the logic of Christianity.

As a response to the question of how it is possible to be a Christian today and to believe as a Catholic, this document, which is quite personal and at the same time quite ecclesial, can be of great help to anyone who is searching.

In the second place, I wish to mention the encyclical *Redemptoris missio*.

This is a document that highlights the lasting importance of the missionary task of the Church, discussing in particular the questions that are posed to Christianity in Asia and that preoccupy theology in the Western world.

It examines the relation between interreligious dialogue and the missionary task and shows how, even today, it is important to proclaim the Good News about Christ, the Redeemer of all mankind, to people from all parts of the world and of every culture.

In the third place, I wish to cite the encyclical on moral problems, *Veritatis splendor*.

It took long years to mature, and its relevance is unchanged today. The Vatican II Constitution on the Church in the Modern World, in contrast to the natural-law orientation of moral theology prevalent at the time, called for a biblical foundation for Catholic moral teaching in terms of the figure of Jesus and his message. Initial attempts at this were made, but only for a short time, and then the opinion gained currency that the Bible had no morality of its own to proclaim but, rather, referred to moral models that were valid at a given time. Morality is a question of reason, they said, not of faith.

Thus, on the one hand, morality understood in terms of natural law disappeared, but no Christian concept of it replaced it. And since it was not possible to recognize either a metaphysical or a christological foundation of morality, people resorted to pragmatic solutions— to a morality founded on the principle of weighing goods, in which good and evil, properly speaking, no longer exist, but only what is better or worse in terms of the effects.

The major task that the pope set for himself in this encyclical was to find once more a metaphysical foundation in anthropology as well as a Christian actualization of it in the new image of man presented in Sacred Scripture.

Studying and assimilating this encyclical is still a major task and an important one.

Of considerable importance also is the encyclical *Fides et ratio*, in which the pope strives to offer a new vision of the relation between Christian faith and philosophical reason.

Finally, it is absolutely necessary to mention *Evangelium vitae*, which is about one of the fundamental themes of the whole pontificate of John Paul II: the inviolable dignity of human life, from the first moment of conception.

What were the prominent features of the spirituality of John Paul II?

The pope's spirituality was characterized above all by the intensity of his prayer, and, therefore, it was profoundly rooted in the celebration of the Holy Eucharist and in praying together with the whole Church in the Liturgy of the Hours.

In his autobiographical book *Gift and Mystery*, we can see how much the sacrament of Holy Orders marked his life and his thinking. Thus his piety could never be merely individual but was also always full of solicitude for the Church and for mankind in general.

The task of bringing Christ to others was anchored at the center of his piety.

We all knew about his great love for the Mother of God. When he dedicated himself totally to Mary, this meant that with her he was there for the Lord totally. Just as Mary did not live for herself but for him, so too he learned from her and from being with her to be completely willing to serve Christ.

Your Holiness, you started the process of beatification before the usual interval established by canon law. Since when and on what basis have you been convinced that John Paul II is a saint?

Again and again during the years of my collaboration with him it became increasingly clear to me that John Paul II was a saint. First of all, of course, I should mention his intense relationship with God, his being immersed in communion with the Lord, of which I have already spoken. That was the source of his joy, in the midst of the great troubles that he had to overcome, and of the courage with which he performed his duties in a truly difficult time.

John Paul II did not seek applause, nor did he ever look around anxiously, wondering how his decisions would be received. He acted on the basis of his faith and his insight and was willing even to suffer blows.

The courage of the truth is in my view a first-class criterion of sanctity.

Only in terms of his relationship with God is it possible to understand also his tireless pastoral commitment. He gave himself so radically that it cannot be explained otherwise.

His commitment was untiring, and not only on his major journeys, with schedules that were crammed with appointments, from start to finish, but also day after day, beginning with his morning Mass until late at night.

During his first visit to Germany (1980), I experienced that enormous commitment for the first time very concretely. For his stay in Munich in Bavaria, I decided that he should take a rather long break at midday. During that interval he called me upstairs to his room. I found him reciting the breviary and said to him, "Holy Father, you ought to rest." He said, "I can do that in heaven."

Only someone who is profoundly imbued with the urgency of his mission can act that way.

But I must also commend his extraordinary kindness and consideration.

Often he would have had sufficient reason to reproach me or to put an end to my appointment as prefect. And yet he stood by me with an altogether incomprehensible faithfulness and kindness.

Here, too, I would like to cite an example. In view of the whirlwind that had developed surrounding the declaration *Dominus Iesus*, he told me that some Sunday at the Angelus he intended to defend the document unequivocally. He invited me to write a statement for the Angelus message that would be, so to speak, watertight and would not allow any different interpretation. It had to be apparent in an entirely unmistakable way that he approved of the document unconditionally.

Therefore I prepared a short speech; I did not want to be too inflexible, however, and so I tried to express myself clearly but without harshness. After reading it, the pope asked me once again: "Is it really clear enough?" I answered Yes.

Anyone who knows theologians will not be surprised by the fact that, all this notwithstanding, afterward it was maintained that the pope had cautiously distanced himself from that document.

How do you feel personally now that the Church is officially recognizing the sanctity of "your" pope, John Paul II, since you were his closest collaborator?

My memory of John Paul II is full of gratitude. I could not imitate him and did not have to, but I tried to carry on his heritage and his task as well as I could. And so I am quite sure that even today his kindness accompanies me and his blessing protects me.

II

In the Pope's Apartment

Stanislaw Dziwisz

"FROM KRAKÓW TO ROME
TO THE GLORY OF THE ALTARS"

On October 16, 1978, Father Stanislaw Dziwisz, like the rest of the world, was waiting for the election of the new pontiff. It was the second time that year that he had accompanied his "Boss", the archbishop of Kraków, to the conclave.

The first time they had had to travel to Rome in August, after the death of Paul VI. On August 6, Cardinal Karol Wojtyła was with friends on vacation in his beloved mountains. The sad news struck him deeply, because he was very attached to the deceased pontiff, in whom he saw a true father and pastor to imitate. Pope Montini, in turn, had greatly esteemed that young Polish cardinal. On August 8, Wojtyła returned to Kraków and three days later left for Rome together with his trusted secretary.

Whenever someone asked Cardinal Wojtyła who would be elected the new pope, he used to answer: "The Holy Spirit will point him out." In the days between the funeral and the beginning of the conclave, Wojtyła met a great many people, among them various prelates.

Father Stanislaw recalls that his "Boss", who was residing in the Polish College on the piazza Remuria, had once invited the patriarch of Venice to dinner. Cardinal Luciani accepted the invitation, and so he too had the opportunity to become acquainted with him; he was impressed then by the great spontaneity of the future pope. During the same period the archbishop of Kraków met Cardinal Joseph Ratzinger, too. On August 25, Father Stanislaw accompanied "his" cardinal to the conclave, which, observers were predicting, would be long and laborious. But the facts belied the predictions: the following day at six in the evening, the white smoke from the Sistine Chapel announced the election of Albino Luciani as supreme pontiff.

Father Stanislaw remained with Cardinal Wojtyła in Italy until September 5. On August 30, the archbishop of Kraków was received by John Paul I in a private audience. On September 1, Wojtyła and Dziwisz went to Turin to visit Archbishop Anastasio Ballestrero (that journey was also an opportunity to pray before the Shroud of Turin); on September 3, the Solemn Mass marking the beginning of the pontificate was celebrated with the traditional respects paid by the cardinals to the new pontiff. On September 5, they took an airplane to Warsaw, and on the sixth, they were once more in the residence of the archbishop of Kraków.

Life seemed to have returned to the way it had been before. Cardinal Wojtyła traveled a lot, and Father Dziwisz accompanied him everywhere. Upon returning from Rome, in that month of September alone, they went to the Shrine of Kalwaria Zebrzydowska, to Tarnów, to Olsztyn, to Katowice, and to Częstochowa. From September 20 to 25, Wojtyła, together with a delegation of the Polish episcopate headed by the primate Stefan Wyszynski, paid an historic visit to Germany. On September 28, Father Stanislaw accompanied the cardinal to the cathedral in Wawel (the castle of the kings of Poland), the same place where, exactly twenty years before, Father Karol Wojtyła had been consecrated a bishop on the feast day of Saint Wenceslaus (*Waclaw* in Polish).

The following day, Father Stanislaw was having breakfast with his bishop when the chauffeur of the chancery, Józef Mucha, entered the room, all excited, and in a tremulous voice said: "John Paul I has died." Wojtyła was upset over the news, and, murmuring: "That is unheard-of, unprecedented ...", he retired to his room. Shortly afterward, the secretary saw him go to the chapel, where he remained for a long time.

Father Stanislaw clearly recalls also the words spoken by the cardinal during the homily of the Mass for the deceased pontiff. They showed his state of soul: "The whole world, the whole Church is wondering: 'Why?' ... We do not know what this death means for the Apostolic See. We do not know what Christ wanted to say to the Church and to the world through this death."

But for the secretary, the death of the Holy Father meant that once again he needed to pack the suitcases and make arrangements to travel to Rome. It was the same situation as in August. But for Karol

Wojtyła, this time it was something different. He was more thought-ful, even though he did not show his feelings.

On October 3, Father Stanislaw landed together with the cardi-nal at Fiumicino Airport; immediately they went to Saint Peter's to pay their respects to the body of Pope Luciani. On October 14, the secretary accompanied Cardinal Wojtyła to the conclave, but first they visited Monsignor Andrzej Maria Deskur, a longtime friend of Wojtyła's, who was recovering at the Gemelli Teaching Hospital from a cerebral hemorrhage. At 4:30 P.M. the conclave began that was to select the 264th bishop of Rome.

Your Eminence, what happened on October 16, 1978?

During the days of the conclave, I, too, went to Saint Peter's Square and waited impatiently in the crowd for the election of the pope. I was there also on the evening of October 16, when Cardinal Pericle Felici pronounced the name of the elected prelate. It was my bishop! It was an immense joy, but at the same time I was left as though paralyzed.

In a flash I remembered when everything had started: exactly twelve years before, one day in October 1966, then-Metropolitan Archbishop of Kraków Karol Wojtyła summoned me to his office.

I was twenty-seven years old then, a young priest: only three years earlier I had received priestly ordination through his hands. During that meeting, he had asked me to help him by accepting the position of personal secretary. While I was still finishing my question, "Start-ing when?", I heard the answer: "Starting immediately!" The next day I went to work.

I did not realize then that I had undertaken the most important adventure of my life. The position of secretary to the archbishop of Kraków was important, no doubt. But I could not foresee the future ramifications of that call; I could not foresee that one day, after twelve years with Wojtyła in Kraków, I would hear on Saint Peter's Square someone pronounce the words: "Habemus Papam, eminen-tissimum ac reverendissimum Dominum, Dominum Carolum, sanc-tae Romanae Ecclesiae Cardinalem Wojtyła, qui sibi nomen imposuit Ioannis Pauli Secundum" ("We have a pope,... Karol Wojtyła, car-dinal of the Holy Roman Church, who has taken the name John Paul the Second").

But according to historians and many men of the Church, that was not such an unforeseeable thing then.

This is true. In Kraków there were many people who were praying that "their" archbishop would not be elected: they did not want to lose him. But it happened.

When did you see your archbishop again, once he had become pope?

I was standing on the square, near the entrance to the basilica. Someone recognized me as Cardinal Wojtyła's secretary and accompanied me to the entrance to the Vatican, which was still closed. As soon as the doors were opened, the Marchese Giulio Sacchetti accompanied me to the room where the pontiff was dining with all the cardinals. Immediately afterward, the Cardinal Chamberlain Jean Villot brought me to the Holy Father.

I was extremely emotional when I saw him wearing white, and he, without speaking, peered intently at me, probably to discover what I was feeling at that moment. Then he approached and whispered to me a remark drawing on his proverbial sense of humor. And so I relaxed: I had understood that, even as pope, he would remain as he was in Kraków.

That same evening, the new pope asked me to be his secretary. I accepted, obviously, but after returning to the Polish College I was wide-eyed until dawn. I could not sleep. In contrast, John Paul II remained at the Vatican: he spent the night in the apartment he had shared with Cardinal Corrado Ursi during the conclave in order to write in Latin his homily for the next day.

Many people noted the great serenity of that "unknown" archbishop of Kraków in facing a task that seemed superhuman, that could have terrified anyone: the job of being pastor of the Universal Church.

As I reflect on this fact, I think that the whole previous life, both personal and priestly, of Karol Wojtyła was a preparation for that unique and extremely difficult mission. He lived in very tough times for the Polish nation: the Nazi occupation, first, and then the Communist regime.

For more than forty years, the Church in Poland had been the one institution that opposed that atheistic system, which was alien to Polish tradition and culture, the one bulwark of defense of human rights, including the right of religious liberty.

In those difficult years, Cardinal Wojtyła upheld the wise, far-sighted policy of the primate of Poland, Cardinal Wyszynski, to save the spiritual identity of the nation.

Where did your cardinal and, then, the pope derive the inspiration and strength to function in such a delicate situation?

I was perhaps the closest witness to the life and pastoral mission of Cardinal Wojtyła. I can testify, and it greatly impressed me, that all of his activity—his meetings with the people, the decisions he made, his pastoral visits, his proclamation of the Word of God, his academic work—was immersed in prayer. Prayer was the center of his life, which only appeared to be frenzied.

To confirm this, I would like to emphasize that the cardinal had placed in the chapel of the archbishop's residence a small table with a lamp and papers. It served as his writing desk: he wrote all his documents, speeches, articles, and books in the chapel: therefore they were the fruits of his encounter with the Eucharistic Jesus.

This encounter with Jesus also instilled in him that great peace and spiritual joy which were evident to everyone and gave him the energy he needed to serve the community of which he was the pastor. And, despite all his duties, he also found time for cultivating friendships and for moments of rest, for trips to the mountains, for skiing.

This same closeness of Jesus was what gave him also the great tranquility he showed in facing the most important challenge of his life. It surprised me, but from the first day he felt at home in the Vatican. He learned very fast to "act like a pope", but in his new mission he always took his previous Polish experiences into account. He was proud of the culture and history both of the Polish nation and also of the Polish Church, which he considered the root of his identity. But the fact that he was profoundly rooted in that Catholic and national culture did not prevent him from being readily open to other cultures, experiences, traditions, and contexts.

Obviously, the pope's solid intellectual and philosophical training, his ability to listen and to reflect, and his knowledge of languages contributed to his truly unique love of neighbor. He knew very well how to read the modern world and the challenges that awaited him, with their opportunities and dangers.

The Polish pope made himself known to the whole world by giving on October 22, 1978, the famous homily of the Solemn Mass for the Inauguration of his Pontificate.

There are many people who, at such a great distance in time, still remember those words: "Do not be afraid. Open wide the doors for Christ! To his saving power open the boundaries of States, economic and political systems, the vast fields of culture, civilization and development. Do not be afraid. Christ knows 'what is in man'. He alone knows it.... Let Christ speak to man. He alone has words of life, yes, of eternal life."

Here already was the entire program carried out subsequently over the course of the almost twenty-seven years of his pontificate.

These words of his show also the character, the faith, and the hope of Karol Wojtyła.

This powerful invitation by John Paul II was cited, significantly, by Benedict XVI on May 1, 2011, during the beatification ceremony for his predecessor, when he said: "What the newly-elected Pope asked of everyone, he was himself the first to do: society, culture, political and economic systems he opened up to Christ, turning back with the strength of a titan—a strength which came to him from God—a tide which appeared irreversible. By his witness of faith, love, and apostolic courage, accompanied by great human charisma, this exemplary son of Poland helped believers throughout the world not to be afraid to be called Christian, to belong to the Church, to speak of the Gospel. In a word: he helped us not to fear the truth, because truth is the guarantee of liberty."

Karol Wojtyła had the strength of a giant, because he was a giant of faith. His service to the Church and to humanity had their origin in faith. From faith sprang his vision of the world and of man, a being created in the image and likeness of God and called to life with God and in God.

John Paul II succeeded in presenting effectively this vision to modern man and in reaching his heart with it, so as to show him that only in God, only in Jesus Christ, does man find the meaning of his life and of his death, sufferings and joys, and the fulfillment of his deepest hopes.

During the Year of Faith, the Synod on the New Evangelization was held in the Vatican; this theme remains a priority in the agenda of Pope Francis. In this context I would like to recall that John Paul II also launched the idea of the "new evangelization" in the homily he gave in Nowa Huta in 1979, during his first apostolic journey to his homeland.

The pope spoke about a new evangelization because he was a great evangelizer. In today's world it is possible to evangelize thanks to authentic witnesses to the faith, among whom we should expect to find genuine pastors in the vanguard.

And John Paul II was at the same time a witness and a pastor. In him personally we received the gift of a wise guide who was capable of guiding the Church and humanity in our difficult, troubled world.

I was a witness (perhaps I should say: "We were all witnesses") of this, his gigantic work of evangelization. Throughout his pontificate, our dear pope did not spare himself, his sole intention being that the truth of Christ—Lord and Redeemer of mankind—should reach everyone: those who have not yet heard tell of him as well as those who have forgotten him in the desert created by secularism, where man lives as though God did not exist.

Your Eminence, it is not possible, in a short conversation like this one, to touch on the particulars of the extremely rich pontificate of John Paul II. Therefore, in conclusion, I limit myself to a more personal question: How do you live out your role as a witness of the sanctity of Pope Wojtyła?

I, as a man and as a priest, was formed in the "school" of Karol Wojtyła. He continues even now to inspire my service to the Church and to the people.

John Paul II wanted me to be the executor of his last will and testament. And I refer particularly to his spiritual testament, because the Holy Father in fact possessed few material things, and those that he had he directed me to give away as gifts. On the other hand, he left an enormous spiritual heritage. I interpret his testament along these lines, and I strive to preserve and to disseminate his intellectual and spiritual heritage, convinced that it can enrich the Church.

For this purpose we are building in Kraków, in the vicinity of the Shrine of the Divine Mercy, the "Have No Fear!" John Paul II Center, which also includes a museum, an institute with its library, a chapel, a place appropriately designed for retreats, a school to train volunteers, an amphitheater, and a hostel.

Thank you for the interview, and I would like to express also my gratitude to you for being a faithful witness to the life and sanctity of Pope Wojtyła.

Emery Kabongo

"HE WAS LIKE THE SERVANT
WHO WENT THROUGH THE STREETS
INVITING EVERYONE TO THE KING'S BANQUET"

When he was elected pope, Cardinal Wojtyła brought with him to the Vatican his Polish secretary, Father Stanislaw, the man who remained at his side until the end of his pontificate.

But John Paul II also had a second secretary; and over the course of twenty-seven years, four different persons succeeded one another in this position. The first was an Irishman, Monsignor John Magee, who was "inherited" from his predecessors Paul VI and John Paul I, to whom he had already rendered service. Monsignor Magee remained in the employ of the Polish pope from 1978 to 1982, when he was appointed master of pontifical liturgical celebrations.

After that, John Paul II selected his secretaries from countries that for one reason or another were especially dear to his heart: by keeping at his side persons from distant regions where the Church was a persecuted minority, the pontiff expressed his closeness to them as universal pastor.

Thus, after Monsignor Magee, he called on an African priest, Monsignor Emery Kabongo from Zaire, who remained with the pope for six years, until 1988. After Monsignor Kabongo left, John Paul II appointed Monsignor Vincent Tran Ngoc Thu, a son of the martyred Vietnamese Church, who served him from 1988 to 1996. The last of the second secretaries was Monsignor Mieczyslaw Mokrzycki, who remained with the pope until his death in 2005; in this volume we will hear from him, too, shortly. But on the following pages we have recorded the testimony of Archbishop Emery Kabongo, today a canon of Saint Peter's Basilica.

Your Excellency, could you recall for us the circumstances in which you became a secretary of John Paul II?

I saw John Paul II for the first time in 1980, during his apostolic journey to Brazil. At that time I was serving as auditor in the apostolic nunciature of that country. I was in my fourth year in Brazil (previously I had worked at the nunciature in Korea). The pope had his lodgings in the nunciature, and my apartment was located not far from his.

The following year I returned to the Vatican to continue my work in the second section of the Secretariat of State (today it is called the "Section for Relations with States"), where I dealt with the problems of the Asian continent. I was living in the International Clergy House.

On February 10, 1982, I received a telephone call from the then-substitute secretary of state, Archbishop Martinez Somalo, who asked me to appear at the Vatican the following day. Since February 11 is a holiday for the Holy See (the anniversary of the Lateran Treaties falls on that day), I wondered whether there was something urgent to attend to. But the substitute was evasive and just kept repeating, "Come, come."

The next day, in the offices of the secretary of state, Archbishop Martinez Somalo informed me that I had been chosen for the special secretariat of the Holy Father.

How did you react to this news?

I started to laugh and asked whether he was joking. But the substitute replied that it was no joke but, rather, a very serious matter.

I wanted to reflect a bit and took refuge in my office, but then I got a telephone call from Father Stanislaw: "Emery, come here", was all he said. I asked then how I should dress, and he answered, "Remain as you are."

Then I went to the apartment of the pope, who showed me in to his office. We spoke a little (he remembered perfectly our meeting in Brazil), and at the end the Holy Father asked me whether I was ready to begin my new job immediately.

And so you moved into the papal apartment, where everyone was Polish: both the first secretary and the sisters. How did you get along in that environment?

It did not take long for me to realize that the persons who, without any particular merits of my own, had chosen me as a close collabo-rator of the pope were kindhearted. And so I reciprocated, offering them my confidence, and, I say this in all sincerity, I was truly happy the whole time I spent with them.

I began to learn and to speak a little Polish, which I used to concel-ebrate Mass (when there were groups from Poland, it was celebrated in the pope's language). And I expedited the office work. It was a lot of work, but in a truly familial atmosphere.

In what language did you speak with the Holy Father?

Usually in Italian, but every so often the pope addressed me in French. Then we spoke in French.

As his secretary, you spent the whole day at the side of John Paul II. What was an ordinary day of the pope like?

John Paul II rose early to pray. At 7:00 in the morning he celebrated Holy Mass in his private chapel, but we used to find him there earlier, kneeling in prayer. After Mass we made our thanksgiving.

The pope then greeted in the library the guests who had partici-pated in the Eucharist. Some of them were invited also to breakfast. We ate at·table but also talked, because for the pope that was the first opportunity of the day to listen to the persons whom he wanted to hear.

At around 9:00, the Holy Father retired to his private study to work, but first he always made a quick stop at the chapel: every time he passed by the chapel, he would go in for a moment of prayer. He remained in his study, which was located in the room from which he appeared for the recitation of the Angelus, until around 10:30 or 10:45, because his official audiences began at 11:00.

The pope then walked down to the second floor of the Apos-tolic Palace, to the official apartment, where he met the prefect of the Pontifical Household, who informed him about the scheduled meetings.

Dinner was served at 1:00 P.M. in the dining room on the third floor. We secretaries had the job of accompanying the guests and seating them. For the pope, this was another opportunity to meet and speak with persons and collaborators whom he wanted to see and consult.

What did John Paul II do in the afternoon?

He used to rest until 3:00 P.M.; at that hour one of the secretaries would bring him the dossiers from the Curia. Every day, during the hour for the midday meal, the ushers appeared at the door of the papal apartment to deliver a large pouch prepared by the Secretariat of State, with all the documents for the Holy Father. And in the afternoon he took a look at everything.

On some days, again after dinner, there were the so-called "scheduled audiences", that is, meetings with collaborators of the Roman Curia: the secretary of state (Monday), the substitute, the secretary for Relations with States, the prefect of the Congregation for the Doctrine of the Faith, the prefect of the Congregation for the Oriental Churches.

Other heads of dicasteries, when they wanted to talk with the pope, would call the prefecture of the Papal Household to set the date for the meeting.

John Paul II used to work until the hour for supper, but first he made another visit to the chapel to pray: his work was always interspersed with prayer. He had supper together with us, the two secretaries. If there were no guests, the television was turned on.

The pope watched television?

Rarely. He did not have a television in his room, and so occasionally he watched in the refectory.

Did the day end there?

Not at all! At 9:00 P.M. we brought him the work for the evening, because for that hour they would send from the Secretariat of State a second pouch of material destined for the Holy Father. After an hour, or an hour and a half, we left him, and he would remain alone in his study. But we know very well that often the pope used to return to the chapel during the night to pray.

Immediately after the election there were rumors that John Paul II did not know enough about the world and that as a pontiff he would be "too Polish". In a short time, however, it became clear that he was a truly universal pastor, who wanted to reach all the particular Churches to the farthest ends of the earth. In a special way Pope Wojtyła had a place in his heart for Africa, of which Your Excellency is a son. What was his connection with the African Church?

John Paul II had all the nations of the world at heart, but he was particularly concerned about the less fortunate peoples such as the Africans (without forgetting the other continents). Recently we published all the speeches given by the Holy Father in Africa or pertaining to Africa: from these texts emerges very clearly how much he cared about that continent and looked forward to positive changes as soon as possible.

What did John Paul II value in African Catholicism, and what, on the other hand, would he have liked to correct?

The Church in Sub-Saharan Africa is young: Christianity took root among us in the colonial period, and it has a little more than one hundred years of history. The Christian message found fertile ground because by nature an African is a very spiritual, believing person.

I would like to emphasize one thing: the Church, in Africa, never limited herself to a spiritual message but always worked for the human development of the people: education, health care, and economic development. John Paul II, in all his journeys to Africa, referred to human rights, to respect for every person, who is created in the image of God and not in the image of the respective tribes (tribalism is one of the evils that afflict the Dark Continent).

In preparing his speeches, the Holy Father often asked the African bishops directly for advice and suggestions, because he wanted to speak about the concrete things that interested the people. This was his method of working, which he applied before visiting other countries, but also before visiting Roman parishes; he would invite to a preparatory dinner his vicar for the city together with the pastors of the parishes to be visited.

What impressed you most about John Paul II?

His attitude toward individual persons. The pope realized that others came to him because they expected him to say something to them; and he knew how to give something to each person.

I was always impressed by how he welcomed people. You could see his joy in meeting others. And he was anxious to put everyone at ease right away. This was one of his personal charisms.

Thus his house in the Vatican was always full of people, because of the desire he had to be with others, to share their life, even during meals and the more relaxing moments of the day.

As a priest what did you learn from the pope?

I saw in him a great apostle of the Divine Mercy. His first two encyclicals, *Redemptoris hominis* and *Dives in misericordia*, are a hymn to mercy.

I was profoundly touched also by his devotion to our Lady. The Belgian and Dutch missionaries who evangelized my country introduced the Rosary prayer, but that was not the true Marian devotion that now, thanks to John Paul II, I perceive as an element of the faith and an essential nutrient for it.

From the pope I also learned adoration of the Most Blessed Sacrament. His way of celebrating Holy Mass, his gestures, his gaze, as though he were seeing something, were for me, as a Christian and as a priest, a great testimony of faith.

I would like to emphasize also the mystical side of the Holy Father, who was formed by reading the great classics (at home he always kept the books of the mystics close at hand), and the importance of prayer, from which he drew the energy for his actions.

Father Stanislaw admonished me from the very beginning of my collaboration: "Nothing is so urgent that you need to disturb the Holy Father when he is praying." All the things of this world had to wait when the pope "was talking" with God.

As you spent so much time at the side of John Paul II, did you ever have the feeling, during his lifetime, that you were dealing with a saint?

For me Karol Wojtyła was a special, extraordinary person. I felt in my heart that he would become a saint and that the Church would recognize him as such. And I said so when I was called to testify during the process of beatification.

Obviously, in order to prove his status, it was necessary to observe the procedures of the Church, as was done, by waiting for the approval of two miracles that occurred through his intercession. These are a "strict obligation" for any Christian whose process of canonization is under way, in order for him to be recognized first as Blessed and then as a saint.

The Church proclaims Blesseds and saints in order to offer Christian models to believers.

John Paul II is a model of how to live out mercy. He addressed all problems, even the most complicated ones, with the spirit of the Mercy of God.

In one of his parables, Jesus tells of the king who plans the wedding feast for his son to which no one comes. Then the king sends his servants into the streets to invite all the people to the wedding.

The Heavenly Father has prepared for us from the beginning of time a banquet, because he wants us to be happy. John Paul II was like the servant of that king who went through the streets of the world inviting everyone to the banquet of God. But in order to participate in the feast, remember that it is necessary to put on "the wedding garment". And the pope explained by his life that this garment was none other than love.

Mieczyslaw Mokrzycki

"HE WAS CONVINCED THAT HE COULD OFFER MANKIND NOTHING BETTER THAN JESUS"

Mieczyslaw Mokrzycki was born in 1961 in Majdan Lukawiecki in Poland. He completed his studies in theology at the Catholic University of Lublin and was ordained a priest in 1987 by the imposition of the hands of Bishop Marian Jaworski, apostolic administrator of the Latin Rite archdiocese of Lviv. (At the time of the Communist regimes, the archbishop resided in Lubaczów, Poland, not in Ukraine.)

In 1991, when the archdiocese of Lviv of the Latins was restored, he transferred to that ecclesiastical district. He studied at the University of Saint Thomas in Rome, where he earned a doctorate in theology.

In the years 1995–1996, he was working at the Congregation for Divine Worship and the Discipline of the Sacraments in the Vatican, until he was called to serve in the special secretariat of John Paul II, becoming the second secretary of the Polish pope until the latter's death in 2005.

"Mietek"—everyone in the Vatican called him by that nickname—remained, afterward, in the papal apartment with Benedict XVI until 2007: on July 16 of that year, Pope Ratzinger appointed him coadjutor archbishop of the archdiocese of Lviv and decided to preside personally at the episcopal ordination ceremony in Saint Peter's Basilica. Thus Archbishop Mokrzycki, after eleven years spent in the service of the popes, left the Holy See and traveled to Ukraine to place himself at the service of the local community of the Latin Rite Catholic Church. But one part of his heart remained in the Vatican by the tomb of John Paul II, truly a Holy Father.

Archbishop Mokrzycki, how did you become a secretary of John Paul II?

I never thought of becoming the pope's secretary! When I finished my studies in Rome in 1995, my ordinary, Archbishop Jaworski, asked me to stay in Italy to work on the beatification process for the Servant of God Archbishop Józef Bilczewski. So that I could live in Rome, they found work for me with the Holy See, in the Congregation for Divine Worship and the Discipline of the Sacraments, and during that time, therefore, I had the opportunity to become better acquainted with John Paul II and Monsignor Stanislaw Dziwisz.

I got along well with the pope immediately, but surely the great friendship between him and Archbishop Jaworski was a factor in my appointment.

Do you remember the moment when the pope asked you to become his secretary?

It was a simple meeting. John Paul II called me into his study and told me: "I would like you to work with me and to help Father Stanislaw. I think that we will get along well together." Forthright words, just the essentials.

You emphasized a moment ago that the pope, in turn, liked you.

That is true. He always put me at ease. When he saw me, he would smile. Every time, in the most varied circumstances, he winked at me as though to say to me: it is all right, everything is under control. I worked with him without anxiety, without stress.

But you worked a lot.

There was so much work that it kept you busy the entire day and you had no time left for yourself.

The pope worked with herculean strength, but then he had a lot of stamina: he used to sleep only six hours. During the day, even when he was traveling, a quarter hour of sleep was enough for him to regain his strength.

Is it true that John Paul II liked to work in his bedroom?

Yes. He had had a desk place in the corner of his bedroom, between two windows; the pope liked to work there.

He would keep the window open, because he wanted fresh air. And on the desk there were always flowers: in the spring, one of the sisters would bring him lilies of the valley, which were so fragrant.

The secretaries of John Paul II shared meals with him, too. What was mealtime like in the papal household?

The Polish sisters who took care of the papal apartment worked in the kitchen, but they cooked in the Italian style.

At dinner there was pasta, meat, and vegetables; at supper, broth or minestrone, with a little meat or sausage.

There was never a lack of pastries: the pope liked them so much. The sisters did not want him to gain weight, but when they played for time at the end of the pasta course and did not serve dessert, John Paul II would start making little circles on the table with his index finger and would smile slyly; that is how he insisted on having his little pastry.

How did you observe the holidays of Christmas and Easter?

The Holy Father was very anxious for us to celebrate the holidays in a family atmosphere, according to the Polish traditions.

For Christmas Eve—besides us members of the household, the secretaries and the sisters—several guests were invited. Cardinal Andrzej Maria Deskur was always there with the sisters, Father Professor Tadeusz Styczen, a few priests who worked at the Vatican, and some old friends of the pope from Kraków together with their families.

John Paul II would begin the evening by lighting a candle at the window. He had started that tradition in 1981, when General Jaruzelski declared martial law in Poland; and Wojtyła wanted that candle to symbolize his closeness to his persecuted people.

Once that gesture was made, there was a reading of a passage from the Gospel, and only then did supper begin: according to the custom, twelve Polish dishes were prepared.

After the supper we sang Christmas carols. The pope liked very much to sing: we did this every evening for the whole Christmas season, until January 6.

In 1982, Pope Wojtyła introduced the tradition of setting up on Saint Peter's Square a monumental presepio (Nativity scene) in the shade of a gigantic Christmas tree.

The Holy Father liked the Christmas tree very much: to decorate the apartment they used to send him little fir trees from the Polish mountains, from Zakopane. And in the corridor a manger scene was set up, "because there can be no Christmas without a *presepio*".

Were there presents under the tree?

No, there were not, because in this respect, too, we followed the Polish tradition, whereby Saint Nicholas brings gifts on December 6.

And so after supper, on that day, Saint Nicholas came into the refectory, announced by bells. It was one of the sisters, dressed up as the "saint of presents". I don't know whether I should be telling you this.

To tell the truth, in my first year in the papal household I was surprised, because to me it seemed to be a holiday for children, and we were all grown-ups. But I was moved by how much the pope cared for us and also because I understood that in those moments he was recalling the memories of his childhood in Wadowice.

Your account is very moving; it tells us about the pope's simplicity of heart. But it also takes us back to the initial happy years of Karol Wojtyła's family; recall that he was born in 1920 and eventually was left almost alone: he lost his mother Emilia at the age of nine, and his father Karol at the age of twenty-one; he had also lost an older sister, Olga, and his brother Edmund in 1932. But please continue telling us about how you celebrated the holiday.

At that point, "Saint Nicholas" had something to say with regard to each person present, before going on to distribute the gifts. Little things: pastries, fruit, a scarf, a shirt, gloves. We joked and laughed.

And it was always like that, every year, until the end, that is, until December 2004.

In contrast, how did you celebrate Easter?

The Holy Father looked forward to Easter all year. His participation was intense and truly special. Holy Week is connected with the Eucharist, with the death and Resurrection of Christ, and therefore John Paul II prepared for it by praying even more; you noticed that he had greater concentration, and he observed the fast very scrupulously.

In those days no guests were invited, because we understood that he needed silence and recollection (the only exception was Holy Thursday, when he used to invite priests from his former archdiocese of Kraków to dinner).

Easter Sunday used to begin, according to Polish tradition, with the blessing of the holiday foods: the painted hard-boiled eggs (*pisanki*), the sausages, the different kinds of cheese, the typical Easter pastries. Finally we exchanged wishes while eating the eggs.

Immediately after the Easter meal, the pope had to celebrate Holy Mass on Saint Peter's Square, did he not?

Yes. It was the most important Eucharistic celebration of the year. And before starting it, the pope, naturally, used to withdraw to pray.

Easter Sunday in 1998—if memory serves me, that was the year—coincided with the beginning of daylight savings time, the day of the transition from the winter schedule to the summer schedule when you set the clocks ahead one hour. But that date had escaped John Paul II, since he was completely preoccupied with Holy Week; and none of us who lived with him had thought to remind him of it in time. That is, before the pope, as usual, went to the chapel immediately after the meal to prepare for Mass in his way.

When he prayed, he was so immersed in profound communion with God that he seemed to forget the outside world.

We members of the household were very conflicted: we were always determined not to interrupt his prayer, and in this predicament, too, we had no intention of doing that; but we wondered with growing apprehension how long he would continue. Besides, the crowds on the square were getting truly worried, and the Easter Mass was to be broadcast worldwide on television. As it turned out, we were twenty minutes late.

Afterward, when we recalled the episode, we always laughed heartily, but at that moment, I can assure you, there was nothing at all to laugh about.

Your Excellency, you have given us some fresh and, I might say, lighthearted tidbits from the life of John Paul II. But between the lines of your account one senses that life with Pope Wojtyła had another dimension, too. Cardinal Dziwisz declared that those who lived close to the pope touched a "mystery". You lived in the papal household for about ten years; do you agree?

In the Scriptures we read that the people who met Jesus wanted at least to touch his garments; and that the first Christians, when Saint Peter would walk by, wanted his shadow at least to graze them. In a very similar way, those who for various reasons came into contact with John Paul II—not only the faithful or the pilgrims, but even we, his co-workers—felt strongly this desire, not to touch him, but to see him, to be near him, to feel his presence "physically".

I had the privilege of meeting with him every day, and every time I had the experience of an interior joy and peace. He transformed every-thing, including me, with his comportment, his prayer, his gestures.

He radiated a great gentleness, because he was a man of God, full of his peace.

Every individual was transformed by meeting with John Paul II, was filled with a grace that came from the Lord through this servant of his. When he was present, everyone felt better, capable of doing good. I think this is the most authentic sign of his sanctity.

Despite the great stature of John Paul II, even during his pontificate there were those who attacked the Church, as always: they disputed his teaching, disparaged his personal history, and ridiculed Christian morality. How did the pontiff react to those attacks?

I think that, humanly speaking, he suffered, but, on the other hand, he was a man of very staunch faith and boundless confidence in the

Lord. He commended everything, problems and worries, however great or little they might be, to the Heavenly Father in prayer. He trusted in God, convinced that he would find the best solution in each matter.

As Vicar of Christ, he was pained by attempts to marginalize the Church and to dispute Christian morality, because he was convinced that there is no better plan of life that can be offered to mankind than the one proposed by Jesus in the Gospel.

But let us stay on the subject of trust: I was struck by his firm conviction that the truth always makes its way and finally will be victorious. Moreover, if any man did not acknowledge the truth, he would deny himself and end up at the mercy of absurdity. This attachment to the truth, this way of understanding life according to the truth, the conviction that his role (like that of Jesus) was to bear witness to the truth, provided him with the perspective with which he looked at and confronted every circumstance.

Your Excellency, while serving the "Polish pope", you became acquainted with Cardinal Ratzinger.

I was acquainted with Cardinal Ratzinger even before I entered the service of John Paul II and met him. Already as prefect of the Congregation for the Doctrine of the Faith he had the reputation of being a great authority and distinguished himself by his profound language, which was nevertheless always clear. And he was admired and studied because of his great love for theology.

After the death of John Paul II, when the new pontiff was elected, Pope Ratzinger approved you for two years as his second secretary, before elevating you to the episcopal dignity: How did you experience the transition from the "Polish pope" to the "German pope"?

Joseph Ratzinger is a very good and humble person and, at the same time, decisive and strong. During his pontificate, too, at the height of his powers, he was always sober in his gestures, because he is discreet and does not want to bully anyone. He has a big heart. As I said, he loved theology, and even as pope he spent a lot of time studying, reading, writing books, and personally preparing his homilies and speeches.

Is there something in particular for which you would like to thank Saint John Paul II?

First of all I would like to thank him because he permitted me to work with him, to stand by the Vicar of Christ, who is Peter in our times. I would like to thank him for the great witness of faith that he gave me day after day; for the cordiality, the humanity, the joy and kindness that he communicated; for teaching me, by his life, how to treat my neighbor and what humility is. Finally, I would like to thank him for his love for the Universal Church.

For me, staying with John Paul II was like attending a school of religious life, spiritual life, and the interior life. He taught me how the Holy Eucharist should be celebrated, how to approach personal and community prayer.

Today I ask him to keep watching over us with his attentive, kind, and tender care, so as to make us feel safe and strong again.

III

Longtime Friends

Andrzej Maria Deskur

"ON HIS DOOR THEY WROTE: 'FUTURE SAINT'"

Immediately after the election of John Paul II, an unexpected thing happened: the new pope went privately, without the great pomp that usually accompanies such events, to the Gemelli Hospital in Rome to visit his friend, who had suffered a stroke. This was the first "journey" of the pope outside the Vatican. On that occasion, he gave a short speech, in which he said among other things: "I came here to pay a visit to my friend and colleague, Bishop Andrzej Deskur, president of the Pontifical Commission for Social Communications, from whom I have received a great deal of affection and friendship and who has been in the hospital in serious condition for several days, since the day before the conclave. I wanted to visit not only him, but all the other patients, too."

In this way the world learned about the friendship between two great Poles: Karol Wojtyła and Andrzej Maria Deskur.

Deskur (born in Sancygniów on February 29, 1924) was a Polish nobleman of French descent. Before the election of the archbishop of Kraków to the See of Peter, he had become one of the most important figures from his country ever to have worked in the Roman Curia.

From 1952 on, his name is connected with the pontifical dicasteries that deal with the mass media (first with the Pontifical Commission for Cinematography, then with the Pontifical Commission for Social Communications, and finally with the Pontifical Council for Social Communications). Having understood the potential of the new means of communications, Monsignor Deskur was one of the most active proponents of introducing the Church to the world of the mass media. He participated in the Second Vatican Council as a theologian and a member of the commission that prepared the conciliar decree *Inter mirifica*, On the Means of Social

Communication. He was one of the founders of the Vatican Press Office. And thanks to his efforts, the first satellite transmission was made and the radio station Radio Veritas was born, which broadcast religious programs to Asia and Oceania.

A great worker and a faith-filled apostle, this tenacious Polish prelate did not like to spare himself; over the years he visited more than seventy countries to sensitize bishops throughout the world to opportunities for modern religious communications.

During that whole time, notwithstanding his ardent endeavors for the Holy See, Deskur always kept in contact with his friend from the seminary, Karol Wojtyła, taking advantage of every visit he made to Rome to meet with him, very often inviting him over to his house.

He had agreed to speak with me about this friendship on the thirtieth anniversary of the election of the archbishop of Kraków to the papacy, which for him coincided with the thirtieth anniversary of the illness that held him prisoner between his wheelchair and his bed. In the following pages I reprint our conversation with the nostalgia that one has for a dear person who is no longer physically among us. Having been created cardinal by John Paul II in the consistory of May 25, 1985, Deskur in fact passed away at the Vatican on September 3, 2011.

Your Eminence, when did you become acquainted with Karol Wojtyła?

I was already acquainted with Karol Wojtyła long ago in 1945 in Kraków. We were studying together in the Metropolitan Seminary: I was in the first year, he was in the fourth. In 1946, news spread that Wojtyła would be ordained a priest and sent abroad to study. It was a great honor, but no one envied him, because everyone wished him well and recognized his great intelligence, solid preparation, and profound spirituality.

During our studies, we lived together and had the opportunity to become acquainted. Everyone competed to go with him during the weekly walks, because one always returned enriched.

One day someone wrote on the door of his room: "Karol Wojtyła: future saint". It seemed to be a joke; actually it reflected the opinion we already had then of the young Wojtyła. And now this incident becomes symbolic. I do not know whether some seminary classmates told this story during the canonical process.

On the evening before his departure, Karol came to me to ask whether it was not risky to send a young priest like him abroad. I told him: "God never runs any risk, because he holds everything in his hand. Do not worry: he holds you in his hand, too."

And so Wojtyła left for Rome. But you, too, Your Eminence, were sent in 1950 first to Fribourg to study moral theology, then to Rome to the Pontifical Ecclesiastical Academy. Afterward you settled in the Vatican, while Karol Wojtyła, after finishing his studies at the Angelicum, returned to Kraków. Did you lose touch with each other?

Not exactly. We met during the sessions of the Second Vatican Council. I was a conciliar theologian; he was a Council Father, first as auxiliary bishop, then as archbishop of Kraków. I participated with him in all the meetings of the commissions of which he was a member. Bishop Wojtyła was highly regarded everywhere, because he had a very remarkable character trait: he was not polemical. It was not possible to quarrel with him, because in his discussions only the arguments mattered.

When Paul VI died, and John Paul I soon afterward, you had already had extensive curial experience and were well acquainted with the cardinals gathered for the new conclave. Did you expect the election of a non-Italian cardinal?

I expected the election not only of a non-Italian cardinal, but of a specific prelate, the archbishop of Kraków.

I would like to explain what I mean: everyone knows that the new pontiff is elected by the cardinals, but in a certain sense his most important elector is his predecessor, too, who chooses the members of the college of cardinals, thus determining the result of the conclave.

Paul VI held Cardinal Wojtyła in great esteem, and I would say that, in a way, he prepared him to be his successor. First, he selected him as preacher of the spiritual exercises at the Vatican, so that the Roman Curia would appreciate his great knowledge and profound spirituality. Then he appointed him relator [the Synod Father who drafts the final report] for the Synod on Evangelization.

It was a surprise for everybody, because they were expecting someone from a mission country. But in this way the Third World cardinals, too, could get to know the Polish archbishop and appreciate his pastoral and missionary zeal.

It is not insignificant, finally, that Pope Montini encouraged Cardinal Wojtyła to travel throughout the world, so as to acquire firsthand knowledge of the reality of the local Churches.

Your Eminence, when John Paul II appeared for the first time on the balcony of Saint Peter's Basilica, you were in a hospital bed at the Policlinico Gemelli: the beginning of your friend's pontificate coincided with your personal tragedy.

I must admit that at the hospital, when I understood that I would remain paralyzed forever, I was shocked.

A paralytic is a person imprisoned by his body, deprived of liberty. Only prayer enabled me to overcome that difficult moment and to accept my infirmity.

When I went back home after the treatments and went into retirement, resigning from the position of president of the Pontifical Council for Social Communications, I received a personal letter from the Holy Father that began with the sentence: "Now you know what your mission in the Church is."

He meant the mission of prayer, the mission of all the sick and the suffering. The pope helped me so much with that letter.

I would like to know whether your illness prevented you from keeping up your close personal relations.

Not at all. Every Sunday I had dinner with the Holy Father in his apartment, and every so often he would come to my place. The Feast of Saint Andrew, my patron saint, was a fixed appointment at my house.

One of the most dramatic moments for John Paul II and his friends was certainly May 13, 1981, the day of the assassination attempt by Ali Agca on Saint Peter's Square. That criminal deed still remains shrouded in secrecy, in terms of the perpetrator and those who sent him.

Few recall that on the evening of May 12, the pope, like all priests, found himself during Evening Prayer reading the passage from the Letter of Saint Paul that says: "Stay sober and alert. Your opponent the devil is prowling like a roaring lion looking for someone to devour."

I consider it obvious that the devil was the one who wanted to "devour" John Paul II, and so the investigation into what physical "hand" and what "instigators" he then used does not matter to me at all.

Satan certainly used the hand of Ali Agca, but it was another hand that deflected the bullet. And that was the hand of our Lady.

John Paul II was convinced of it; during his second stay in Gemelli Hospital in the month of July 1981, he had them bring him the envelope with the original text of the "third secret" of Fatima written by Sister Lucia, since he understood the coincidence between the day on which they had attempted to kill him and the anniversary of the first apparition of the Blessed Virgin. From that day on, when speaking about the attempt, the pope always used to say: "One hand fired and another guided the bullet."

John Paul II did not want you to be unemployed and appointed you president of the Pontifical Academy of the Immaculate Conception. What task did he entrust to you?

The Pontifical Academy of the Immaculate Conception deals with studies of Marian dogmas and devotion, but also with pastoral work.

John Paul II thought so much of the academy because one of his priorities was to revive in the Church the worthy veneration of the Mother of God, whose cult was weakened by an erroneous interpretation of the teachings of the Second Vatican Council.

In the second place, the Holy Father was convinced that the new evangelization, too, necessarily had to pass through the Marian shrines.

Europe has always been the "land of our Lady", dotted with her shrines and centers of spirituality that are dedicated to her.

I remember the words of Karol Wojtyła when he was still archbishop of Kraków: "The Marian shrines are a treasure of the Church, because they are places where the Word of God is proclaimed and the sacraments are administered; they are centers for prayer and for gatherings of the faithful in a broader context than the parish; they are places where the experiences of the pilgrims intertwine with the mystery of Mary, and the experiences of the nation of the homeland, of the region, encounter the love of the Church and of her Mother."

Your Eminence, for nine years you were a member of the Congregation for the Causes of the Saints. John Paul II was accused of proclaiming too many saints and Blesseds. How did the Holy Father respond to such criticisms?

When I brought that objection to his attention, he calmly replied that the Church existed precisely to generate, to raise up saints. There is never enough sanctity in the Church!

For many people John Paul II was "santo subito", a "saint immediately".

The Church has her procedures for canonization, and it is good that they exist, but I always keep in mind the writing over the door of the young seminarian in Kraków: "Karol Wojtyła: future saint".

Stanislaw Grygiel

"THE POPE WHO LOOKED TO THE LAITY, THE FRIEND IN WHOM I RECOGNIZED GOD'S FAITHFULNESS"

The laity had a very special role in the life and formation of Karol Wojtyła. In Kraków, the future pontiff was actively concerned about the pastoral care of youth, then of families and intellectuals. In that setting were born friendships that were to last forever, even after the archbishop of Kraków was elected to the See of Peter.

Especially fraternal was the bond that was established over the years between Wojtyła and Professor Stanislaw Grygiel. Grygiel, who earned a graduate degree in Polish philology at the Jagiellonian University in Kraków and a doctorate in Christian philosophy at the Catholic University of Lublin, has lived since 1980 with his family in Rome, where for many years he was professor of philosophical anthropology at the John Paul II Pontifical Institute at the Pontifical Lateran University, while holding also a position as visiting professor at the same institute in Washington, D.C.

A close friend of Karol Wojtyła from their youth until the latter's death, Professor Grygiel is the right person to ask about the value that the new saint attributed to friendship and with whom to discuss the attention the pope paid to the laity in the Church.

John Paul II gave tremendous encouragement to the recognition of the role of the laity in the Church—an attitude that is already evident in the pastoral activity of Karol Wojtyła when he was a priest and, subsequently, a bishop in Kraków. You, Professor, are a witness of this, since you were connected to the future pope by long-standing ties of friendship.

The life and the work of a man depend not only on him but also on the *humus* or soil in which he finds himself, which is made up of history, the environment, and the culture.

Much has been said already about Polish history and culture, without which it is not possible to understand either the person of John Paul II or his pastoral activity. On the other hand, little is known about the setting in Kraków, with the persons who were decisive for his life.

First of all, it is necessary to recall the figure of Jan Pietraszko, the great bishop, today Servant of God, who showed the young priest Wojtyła the way that leads to young people. John Paul II himself testified to this in the telegram he sent to Kraków upon the death of the bishop: "You opened for me the path that leads to them." I recall a supper hosted by the pope and attended by Bishop Pietraszko. The latter had brought him a copy of his lastest book as a gift. At a certain point the Holy Father told him: "Bishop Jan, I am learning theology from you." Pietraszko was rather perplexed, and as he left the papal apartment, he asked me and my wife: "Tell me, did he say that seriously, or was he joking? My books are for parish priests!" But the pope, the pastor of the whole world, had not been joking. Bishop Pietraszko was one of the greatest teachers of the faith in the Polish Church of the twentieth century. In my view, he is a true Father of the Church.

Of what did the pastoral method of Bishop Pietraszko consist?

It had no conceptually developed method. To put it simply, he was always with us young people, not only in church. He prayed with us, dined with us, meditated and took recreation with us. Looking at him, we saw a fascinating way of being in the world. Being fascinated, we looked for the spring from which he, on his knees, drew water. From a priest who is not on his knees, it is possible to learn to drink fancy, artificial beverages from the bottle, but never pure spring water.

John Paul II and Bishop Pietraszko were the ones who made us see how culture consists of knowing how to cultivate the earth on which man grows and matures "so as to rise again", to use the expression of C.K. Norwid, a great Polish poet whom they often quote. Culture, they tell us, cannot be reduced to learning. On the contrary, nothing is more dangerous to society than learned men who are without culture. Because only culture is life-giving, because the purpose of culture is "to rise again". Culture is either paschal or it is not culture.

This being together was the origin of a deep friendship, one of those friendships that lasts forever; and not merely between them and us, but also among ourselves. In this friendship, the help, or if you prefer, the pastoral work was reciprocal. Wojtyła and Pietraszko helped the young people, and the young people helped them to seek God and to walk toward him. Our bishops were perfectly aware of the fact that the farmer grows and matures together with the plants entrusted to his care.

Among friends there are no barriers, and those two were always accessible and available for us. We could go visit them whenever we wanted. You could knock on their door even at night. The sheep do not request audiences with their shepherds; they follow them day and night. If they are not in a position to do that, it is a sign that they are sheep without pastors.

You spoke about the pastoral ministry of young people, but the future pope was concerned also about families, students, intellectuals.

I said that the two bishops grew and matured at the same pace as the young people. But those young people married, and consequently they [the bishops] had to learn to be with their spouses and, then, with their children, also, whom they considered their "spiritual grandchildren".

Father Wojtyła began his pastoral work with the young altar servers in the parish of Saint Florian in Kraków. But as time went on, those young students turned into professors, physicians, lawyers. And as had already happened to the older Pietraszko, he too considered himself "compelled" to provide pastoral care for the adult professionals he was now facing.

In this way, by extending their own pastoral work, our two bishops had the opportunity to understand from the source, from the living reality instead of from books, what the term "laity" means. Most importantly, they drew "from the source" the truth about marriage and the family.

Is it not possible to teach these things in the seminary?

You learn to live by living; you learn to do by doing. The problem is whether the superiors of the seminary live or know how to live together with the seminarians; whether they are able to cultivate the ground on which they themselves have the opportunity to grow and mature with the seminarians. Pastoral ministry is not a theory but a form of common life. The theories are supposed to be committed to memory, whereas pastoral ministry requires the wisdom that is born in men who are present to each other. Knowledge of the theories can even be an obstacle to the reciprocal presence of the persons; that is, the theories about pastoral ministry can destroy pastoral ministry itself. You can discuss pastoral ministry and plan conferences and publish many documents, but true pastoral ministry is the exchange of gifts between the priest and the lay faithful. Wojtyła understood this very well.

In what way did the lack of religious freedom in Communist Poland influence the pastoral ministry of the Church?

By denying the Church any form of public activity, the Communist regime had compelled her to live in strictly personal relations. Paradoxically, we had to hide our "being together", since the police were doing everything they could to try to prevent it and destroy it.

But thanks also to this dynamic, in that semi-clandestine state, the relations of friendship and mutual trust became stronger and stronger and revealed to us the beauty of the Church, which made us free from everything that is bound up with mere ownership. Thus God made use of and still makes use of those who deny him.

You learned in Kraków that the cardinals assembled in conclave had chosen "your" archbishop, and from Poland you followed the first months of Wojtyła's pontificate. What impact did the election of Karol Wojtyła have on the life of Polish Catholics?

I can only repeat things that have been said again and again. The first reaction of the Poles was joy, but this was immediately followed by

STANISLAW GRYGIEL   63

an awareness of the new opportunities that had opened up that day
for their homeland and for their Church.

The Poles understood that from then on the Church would no longer have to conduct her essential pastoral work in semi-underground
conditions. Catholics became more courageous and bolder: an eloquent sign of this were the popular demonstrations in the streets of
the country that lasted the entire night of October 16, 1978, without
anyone having requested permission.

I recall the discussions with friends in those hours: we were convinced that our borders would be open to the West and that, sooner
or later, Poland would also emerge politically from the Communist
bloc. Until then it was thought that Communism would last for generations, since it was clear to everyone how Western intellectuals and
politicians allowed themselves to be seduced by the words and the
money of the Soviet secret police: how many times, indeed, they, of
all people, had tried to convince us that we had to adapt to Communism! But with the first pilgrimage of the Holy Father to Poland in
1979, the prospects changed all at once, radically.

The pope was able to reawaken in the Poles the hope that had
been lulled by more than forty years of Communism. In the first
years of his pontificate, little by little it became clearer that a new era
was dawning, and not just for Poland.

*Could you explain to us now how John Paul II was able to transfuse into
his Petrine Magisterium all the wealth of his pastoral, cultural, and political
experiences in Poland?*

In Rome, Karol Wojtyła continued to be a man and a priest "with
others", exactly as he had been in Kraków. He changed nothing of
his own behavior. He was not overbearing with anyone, and, on the
other hand, he did not close himself off in what we could describe
as "papal isolation". Therefore, he was able to assimilate the faith,
hope, and love of all the persons whom God entrusted to his pastoral
work, so as then to appreciate and express these gifts with the special
strength of Peter's faith, hope, and love.

John Paul II did not pronounce condemnations; he simply pro-
fessed the Church's faith, expecting that everyone would come to

mature, and he with them. For Wojtyła, human freedom was a *res sacra* (something sacred), and this concept was the result of what he had lived through in the shadows of the occupation of Poland by the Germans, first, and then by the Russians.

Looking to the future of the Church, he took every opportunity to meet with married couples and families. And I consider prophetic his decision to found the Pontifical Institute for Studies on Marriage and Family, which is part of the Pontifical Lateran University.

Those who were accustomed to the isolation of the popes were downright scandalized to witness the overturning of the barriers once set up as a symbol of the Petrine dignity.

John Paul II wrote a large number of documents. It was not the written word, however, that he sought to give to others; rather, he did everything in such a way that his life became a word, as God himself had intended it for others in choosing him as Pastor. I think that pastoral work is often suffocated by too much paper: being a pastor means "pasturing", that is, being with the flock. Christ did not write even one line. He is the living pastoral letter sent to us by the living God. *He* remains with us, not some document of his. To living men, God sends living men. He is not God of the dead (cf. Mt 22:32).

How is it that John Paul II devoted himself so much to the promotion of lay movements?

Because he saw the Church as a great, primordial movement. Already in Poland he had had the opportunity to become acquainted with several movements. Representatives from various movements, in particular from Communion and Liberation, from *Notre Dame de Vie* (Our Lady of Life) and from the Focolari movement, came to us secretly from the West. The metropolitan of Kraków cultivated intense relations with them. I remember in particular the figure of Father Francesco Ricci from Forlì, a disciple of Father Luigi Giussani. Three years after his death, John Paul II told me: "I pray for Father Francesco Ricci every day, during Mass."

In Cardinal Wojtyła's opinion, every parish ought to have a movement. Otherwise, it was not a living parish. For him, an ecclesial movement was any group of persons united in the Eucharist, celebrated by a priest. Without the presence of the Eucharist, movements would be indistinguishable from political parties.

Those who had the good fortune to be guests of John Paul II noticed a family atmosphere in the pope's apartment. The pontiff was surrounded not only by secretaries, sisters, and co-workers, but also by many old friends who frequently visited the papal apartment, often accompanied by family members. Your family was one of the ones most often hosted. What do you remember about those meetings?

The simplicity of the pope's kindness. Conversations with him were exchanges of gifts: he gave us the presence of his person, and we, in receiving it, had the sense of having given him ours. He looked forward to other people and sought them out. He was a man for others. He was a faithful friend.

And it is precisely thanks to this fidelity of his, which was an essential trait, and through his sharing with so many fiancées, married couples, fathers, and mothers, that he completely understood the truth of that covenant which two persons make forever in love.

Moreover, he gave of his time with equal consideration for everyone, whether they were adults or children. Once, when we were his guests at supper, my son, then only eight years old, started kicking me under the table to tell me that he wanted to go back home. The Holy Father noticed it and asked him: "What is the matter?" To which my son unceremoniously replied: "I'm bored. I want to go home." And the pope said: "You are right. I invited you over, and now I am not paying attention to you. You must excuse me." From that moment until the end of the evening he began to play and joke with him.

For me it was a lesson about what it means to live for one's neighbor and to be a pastor.

What do you miss the most about John Paul II?

I don't miss anything except, once in a while, his physical presence. Everything that was essential and special about his person is still present to me. His death destroyed nothing. Our conversation continues. At the heart of the Church, that is, in the Eucharist, there are no dead.

Stanislaw Nagy

A CLOSE FRIENDSHIP THAT STARTED IN A TRAIN
ON THE KRAKÓW-LUBLIN LINE

On September 28, 2003, John Paul II announced the ninth consistory of his pontificate to elevate thirty men of the Church to
the rank of cardinal. Among the prelates to receive the purple hat,
besides well-known leaders of the Curia and of metropolitan arch-
dioceses, the pope named three who were not well known to the
media: Gustaaf Joos, Tomas Spidlik, and Stanislaw Nagy, a Belgian,
a Czech, and a Pole.

In this way, he continued the tradition whereby he rewarded several elderly scholars for their meritorious work in the field of theology. In previous consistories, in fact, John Paul II had appointed
the theologians Yves Congar, Alois Grillmeier, Avery Dulles, and
Leo Scheffczyk.

Among the new cardinals, Nagy was the person whom the pope
knew best and to whom he was connected by strong, long-lasting
personal ties. This priest of the Sacred Heart of Jesus was born in
Silesia (in Bierun, on September 30, 1921) and had studied, like Karol
Wojtyła, at the prestigious Jagiellonian University in Kraków and,
later on, at the Catholic University of Lublin, which at the time of
the Communist regime was the only Catholic college on the other
side of the Iron Curtain. Nagy was affiliated with that prestigious
institution for his whole life, teaching fundamental theology and the
theology of ecumenism.

That was where he became acquainted with his illustrious colleague. The acquaintance between the two men lasted over the years
and solidified into friendship, despite the distance caused by the new
responsibilities to which Wojtyła was called from time to time.

I had the good fortune to meet Cardinal Nagy and to have him
tell me about his relationship with the new saint shortly before the

STANISLAW NAGY   67

former's death, which carried him off at the age of ninety-two, in Kraków, on June 5, 2013.

Your Eminence, the story goes that you and Cardinal Wojtyła became traveling companions on the night train from Kraków to Lublin. Is that true?

We had become acquainted even before he became archbishop, when both of us were teaching at the Catholic University of Lublin. But it is true that for a long time we traveled together from Kraków to Lublin. Since both of us had duties in Kraków and also in Lublin, we used to take the night train so as not to lose time. These trips gave us a good opportunity to discuss things and to get to know each other.

Your Eminence, in what fields did you collaborate with Cardinal Wojtyła?

We collaborated on various occasions. For example, during the two synods of the Church of Kraków: I was responsible for the theological section and therefore had to remain in continual contact with the cardinal. But even earlier we had reason to meet frequently during the work of the Second Vatican Council, in which Bishop Wojtyła participated from the start. I was teaching fundamental theology, and, having had philosophical training, I was at that time better versed in the ecclesiological problems that he had to deal with at the Council. Very often we exchanged ideas, and I benefited by learning what was happening at Vatican II.

But I could recall another fact here, too: after Wojtyła was consecrated a bishop, he had to give up a lot of his duties, among them pastoral assistance to health care workers, which he liked so much. He asked me to take on that duty, which I performed under the sympathetic and watchful eye of the new auxiliary bishop of Kraków.

What was the role of the archbishop of Kraków in opposition to the Communist regime?

The Communist regime aimed to create divisions in the Polish Church and tried to pit the primate, Cardinal Wyszynski, against Cardinal Wojtyła. At first the regime perceived the archbishop of Kraków as a dynamic pastor who was not much interested in politics and, therefore, a much less dangerous person than the archbishop of Warsaw.

That was an enormous error in judgment; moreover, in this way the regime promoted the creation of two leaders of the anti-Communist opposition.

In fact, Cardinal Wojtyła was completely dedicated to the cause of the homeland and of the Polish Church and became public enemy number one of the Communists in the second half of the sixties, when the elderly primate proved to be less active, for personal reasons. Therefore, the regime was genuinely shocked when Wojtyła was elected pope.

In Poland in those days, did anyone expect the election of the archbishop of Kraków to the See of Peter?

Some people were thinking about it, but as an exceedingly optimistic outcome and not that seriously. Cardinal Primate Wyszynski hoped for it with all his heart but did not really expect that Wojtyła would be elected.

Personally I was convinced that another Italian prelate would be chosen, because I thought that the Italian "wellspring" had not yet dried up and that the local Church would coalesce in finding a worthy candidate.

Did you keep up your personal relationship with your friend even after 1978?

The election of Cardinal Wojtyła was for me a tremendous surprise and a pleasant one. But at the time I thought our relationship would no longer be as it was before.

I was wrong. I could not participate together with the other priests of Kraków in the Solemn Mass for the inauguration of the pontificate, and the pope sent me a letter, written in his own hand, in which he told me that he would like to meet with me as soon as possible.

Of course I did not make him wait. And our contacts were never interrupted.

Among other things, another opportunity for collaboration presented itself, since I became a member of the International Theological Commission by papal appointment. The Holy Father was intensely interested in the projects of this commission, so he often called me to talk about the matters that were discussed.

Lastly, in the final years of his pontificate, the pope wanted me to be with him at Castel Gandolfo, and I regularly spent a few weeks of my summer vacation with him.

During your philosophical and theological conversations, did you ever quarrel?

Let us say that it happened every so often that "the theologian from Lublin" and the Holy Father had different opinions. I limit myself to recalling our "quarrel" about the project for the new *Catechism of the Catholic Church*: I thought it would be difficult to accomplish, but he was enthusiastic about it. And he was right.

Everyone who participated in the Holy Mass of John Paul II in his private chapel was impressed. I myself have recorded many testimonies to that effect. What made this celebration of the Holy Father so meaningful?

Every time I was in Rome I concelebrated with the pope.

For John Paul II, the Eucharist was a great mystery, which he experienced very intensely at every stage of it. During his illness, when he celebrated Holy Mass, despite serious problems with his legs and the fatigue of a body that had gained weight and no longer responded well, he never stopped kneeling down: those were truly heroic gestures, which make you understand what he thought about the Eucharist. Personally I never saw anyone else experience the Mass that way.

You mentioned the pope's illness. From the early 1990s, his personal demeanor was profoundly marked by suffering. How did that influence his pontificate?

The reflections of John Paul II about suffering are summarized in the apostolic letter *Salvifici doloris*.

He reacted to his sufferings with great heroism and in the spirit of total acceptance of God's will. I never once saw him become annoyed or complain because of his suffering. Furthermore, his weighty health problems did not diminish his total commitment to carrying out the mission of Peter.

Your Eminence, you are considered to be one of the most illustrious Polish theologians. Does your appointment to the cardinalate have something to do with the prestige that you gained by your writings?

I cannot answer that question exactly; but I can imagine that, since I was not a bishop and had no great pastoral accomplishments, the Holy Father decided to make me a cardinal because of my work as a theologian.

Is it true that, after receiving news of your nomination, you "hid" in the chapel?

I learned about my nomination at seven o'clock in the morning on the day of the official announcement made by the pope.

The news took me by surprise, and furthermore it upset me. And the chapel seemed to me to be the best place to reflect on it, in prayer. Then, at noon, I had the pleasure of receiving congratulations from the cathedral chapter of Kraków.

What did the pontificate of John Paul II mean for the Polish Church?

Karol Wojtyła was a great patriot; you can say that from his childhood he grew in love of his homeland. He testified to his feelings for Poland in the book *Memory and Identity*, which was published shortly before his death. The pope never hid his Polish roots, starting with the famous speech at the beginning of his pontificate when he said: "I came from a distant country."

As pope, he felt responsible also for the Church of which he once was bishop.

Obviously, his feelings for Poland did not limit his love for the whole Church and, particularly, for the poor of the world. All these feelings sprang from his way of understanding the mission of Peter: being the servant of the Church and of all humanity.

Is there anything from the pontificate of John Paul II that is already part of the history of the Church?

In my judgment, these are the aspects of the pontificate of John Paul II that have already gone down in history: the great importance that he assigned to collegiality in the Church; his boundless love for young people; his important doctrinal contribution (the encyclicals, which are theologically rich but, at the same time, rooted in the reality of the world); his missionary activity connected with his apostolic journeys; his struggle for peace; his great project of leading the Church into the Third Millennium (and the pope did so by promoting the memorable event of the great Jubilee of the Year 2000).

Wanda Półtawska

STORY OF A SPIRITUAL FRIENDSHIP

What did the Polish students at the girls' high school in Lublin dream about long ago in 1939? Probably about everything that girls of the same age dream about today: happiness, pretty clothes, evenings at the cinema or the theater, dances, love, kisses and cuddling, the warmth of a home, excursions with friends. But the Nazi insanity robbed that generation of young people of their dreams and happiness, turning their lives into an inferno that lasted for five endless years.

When the German armies invaded Poland on September 1 of that year, thus starting the Second World War, Wanda Wojtasik (that was Mrs. Półtawska's maiden name) was seventeen years old and attended the academy of the Ursuline Nuns in Lublin, in southwest Poland.

She was in charge of a group of scouts. Scouting was a genuine school of living that taught Christian virtues and love of country. It was not surprising, then, that the young lady decided to join the Polish underground resistance (the Association of Armed Struggle). Unfortunately, in February 1941, she was discovered, arrested, and incarcerated for months in the terrible Lublin prison: although mistreated, she divulged no names of her companions in the resistance. In September 1941, she was transported, together with other Polish women, to the concentration camp in Ravensbrück. Beyond the prison gate, she ceased to be a person with a proper name: she became detainee number 7709.

Ravensbrück is a little town in the German region of Mecklenburg, located on the shore of Lake Schwedt. In that countryside, which in itself is idyllic, the German Nazis built one of their "death factories". During the war years, in that camp 130,000 women from twenty-seven nations were imprisoned; out of forty thousand Poles, only eight thousand survived. The prisoners in Ravensbrück, undernourished and exposed to the cold, were compelled to labor in inhumane conditions, and when they could no longer do so, they were tortured and shot. The crematorium in the camp was regularly in use: the ashes of the prisoners were thrown into the waters of the placid lake, which became the tomb for tens of thousands of women.

Wanda was not shot; a crueler lot befell her: she became a *Kaninchen*. This word in German means "rabbit", but in Ravensbrück it had a dreadful connotation: a *Kaninchen* was a prisoner destined to undergo experimental operations by the medical team of the nearby clinic for the SS, headed by Doctor Karl Gebhard. The experiments had to do with new drugs designed to cure infections resulting from the wounds of the soldiers at the front. The prisoners were deliberately wounded and infected with bacteria. In some lacerations, pieces of wood or cloth were also introduced in order to cause gangrene. At that point, the human guinea pigs were treated with the new drugs so as to test their effectiveness. Other experiments involved the process of regeneration of bones, muscles, and nerves and the possibility of transplanting bones from one person to another: some women underwent amputations, others "merely" fractures and lesions.

Wanda was one of the seventy-four Polish women used as guinea pigs. They operated on her legs, and that "experimental" intervention caused her atrocious sufferings: she was on the point of going mad and even harbored the thought of throwing herself against the electrified barbed wire fence to end it all. The *Kaninchen* were all supposed to be eliminated, but the other prisoners fought heroically in defense of their companion, and finally the Germans decided to spare her.

The camp was liberated by Soviet soldiers on April 30, 1945, and Wanda was able to return to Lublin, on foot and by fortuitous means of transportation. But she could no longer remain there: every corner of her city reminded her of her friends and acquaintances who had died during the war. And that was unbearable for her: and so the woman decided to move to Kraków. But the change of residence did not dispel the demons connected with her imprisonment: she had horrible dreams; whenever someone asked who she was, she used to answer automatically: "Number 7709."

In view of the Holocaust, many, many Jews asked themselves where God had been while they were dying; Wanda, after her experiences in the Nazi inferno, asked herself: "Who is man?"

A friend of hers, a woman, advised her to write a book to "work out" the interior drama that was tormenting her: that was the origin of her concentration camp memoirs entitled *And I Am Afraid of My Dreams* (published in English by Hodder & Stoughton). "Yet neither medical studies nor philosophy, not even marriage and family life were able to set my troubled mind at rest and to give valid answers to my questions." Until she met a man, a priest who was able to understand her.

Doctor Półtawska, how did your intense spiritual relationship with Karol Wojtyła begin?

One day I went to Saint Mary's Basilica [in Kraków]. I started to pray, as usual, in front of the large crucifix, when Father Karol Wojtyła entered the church. I had already met him, because he was involved in pastoral assistance to physicians. I watched him kneel down and then go into the confessional. At that point I felt that I had to go to him, as though I were being driven by an interior force. I went to confession.

I still feel the sense of relief and peace that I experienced. After so many quarrels and misunderstandings with many people, even some of goodwill, finally I had found someone who truly understood me.

After my confession he told me: "Come tomorrow morning to Mass. Come every morning." I immediately understood that he was a holy priest, with a rare ability to listen. That is why Father Wojtyła became my confessor and my spiritual director.

What was the pastoral method of Karol Wojtyła?

He asked me to meditate on Sacred Scripture. Every morning, after the Holy Eucharist, I prepared for myself a passage from the Bible. During the day I would meditate on the text and wrote down my reflections; then he read everything and added his comments.

Documents of this sort occupy a substantial part of the book that I dedicated to him. They show the pastoral approach of Father Wojtyła.

Your relationship with Father Wojtyła was not only spiritual but also professional.

That is correct. I was then a young psychiatrist employed by a counseling service for young people. I was consulted also by many couples in crisis who were looking for help.

I soon realized that I needed the counsel and support of a priest. Father Wojtyła was involved in this sort of pastoral ministry and began to help me. This work in common created a strong "professional" tie between us.

Doctor Póltawska, you collaborated with Karol Wojtyła in the field of defending human life and the family. What caused you to be sensitive to these issues?

During my imprisonment at the Ravensbrück camp, I saw the Nazis throw newborns into the crematoria, and all my life those heartrending images have remained before my eyes. For that reason I promised myself then that, if I survived, I would study and defend human life.

As I have already related, Wojtyła was in charge of pastoral care to the physicians, and I was a young doctor: that is how we met.

In 1956, in Communist Poland, the law on abortion was passed. I, as a physician, and he, as a priest, were alarmed by this anti-life decision. And we started to work together in opposition to that law.

We made every effort then to save every single newborn child, every life that was still blossoming, and we went forward from there along that path. In 1967, with the help of Cardinal Wojtyła, I organized in Kraków the Theological Institute for the Family that I then headed for thirty-three years.

John Paul II went down in history also as the pope of the theology of the body. When did Karol Wojtyła become interested in that topic?

Wojtyła was always concerned about anthropology. And in this context he was interested in the love between a man and a woman and in the sanctity of the family.

He insisted so much on the family, because the personality of every human being is—or rather ought to be—formed precisely in the family. At the same time he realized that love, in a family, depends on the correct understanding of the corporeal aspect of the relation between man and woman.

In Kraków, I collaborated with him in the drafting of the book *Love and Responsibility*. In 1979, when he was already pope, he started a series of catecheses on human love in the divine plan, but the text of these reflections had already been completed previously in Poland: he just divided it into a series of catecheses.

And let us not forget that Wojtyła made his great contribution to the preparation of the encyclical *Humanae vitae* by Pope Paul VI.

After becoming pope, Wojtyła wrote to you in a letter dated December 24, 1978: "You were and still are for me my personal expert in the field of Humanae vitae. *So it has been for more than twenty years, and it is necessary to continue." One might say that the contribution made by Wojtyła during the preparation of the encyclical is yours also. Moreover, in the letter just quoted, the pope asks you to "keep reporting" to him "everything that happens in this field".*

And I continued to do so, as he wished.

Your fight to defend human life made you a few enemies: you became the "black sheep" of the Polish feminists, and in certain circles they do not forgive you for comparing the tragedy of abortion and the Holocaust.

How, though, can certain feminists in Parliament wave the banner of women's liberation and, at the same time, condemn to death in their mother's womb the most defenseless beings in the world?

Let us never forget that the number of abortions performed at the global level is terrible and far surpasses the number of victims caused by all the wars ever fought.

1962 was very painful for you, Doctor Póltawska: that year you discovered that you had cancer. A dramatic development, but also miraculous.

When Bishop Wojtyła was in Rome for the Vatican Ecumenical Council II, I felt ill. The bishop was informed, with a telegram from my husband, that I had been admitted to the hospital. Thereupon he—at the suggestion of his friend, Monsignor Deskur—turned to Padre Pio of Pietrelcina. In a letter he asked the friar with the stigmata to pray for a sick woman, without mentioning my name.

Obviously, at that time, I, like everyone else in Poland, knew nothing about that Capuchin religious: the Communists kept us well isolated from the West. Only after I was cured did I find out about that letter (Father Karol wrote a second letter ... of thanksgiving), and I shivered when I learned the contents of it.

To tell the truth, my total and inexplicable cure, instead of making me kneel down to thank the Lord, provoked a sort of rebellion within me: I was frightened by God's power and by the fact that we depend totally on him.

In that way, however, you had the good fortune and the privilege of knowing two saints: Padre Pio and John Paul II. What did these two great men of God have in common?

They combined the great faith and the clear ideas characteristic of those persons who act under the inspiration of the Holy Spirit. They were uncompromising in their principles, cordial, and gentle toward the needy.

Both are models of humility and obedience to God and the Church. Then, too, prayer was extremely important in the lives of both men: Padre Pio founded his famous prayer groups; for John Paul II, prayer was as essential as breathing. He once told me: "People do not realize what a powerful weapon prayer is"; and he always added: "Learn to pray."

I would like to emphasize also that they were both Marian saints, particularly sensitive to the message of Our Lady of Fatima and therefore committed to the salvation of all souls.

Did the people in Kraków who knew Cardinal Wojtyła expect that he would become pope?

In Poland, everyone knew that our archbishop maintained good contacts in the Vatican and was highly esteemed by many cardinals. Moreover, Pope Paul VI called him to preach the spiritual exercises for the Curia: this was an important choice.

For us, 1978 was a special year: my family and I were spending our vacation in the mountains together with Cardinal Wojtyła. On August 6, during breakfast, he confided to us: "I never dream anything, but last night I dreamed that Paul VI was signaling to me." That same morning we learned from the radio about the death of Pope Montini. *Brat* (Brother) remained with us until August 8, when he left for Rome via Warsaw. He returned to Poland at the end of the conclave that led to the election of Cardinal Albino Luciani.

But in September came the surprising news of the death of the new pope, also. When we met in late September, he told us: "I was hoping to have more time." While saying goodbye, I asked him: "What name will you choose as pope?" My husband answered for him: "Obviously: John Paul II." He, in contrast, did not say a word.

He departed from Kraków on October 8, and our next encounter took place in Rome, when he was already John Paul II. I would like to add that many, many years ago my mother had "prophesied" that he would become pope.

One of the distinctive traits of Karol Wojtyła was his faithfulness in friendship. On October 20, 1978, just a few days after his election—we can only imagine how demanding those first steps of his pontificate were—Wojtyła found the time to write you a long, moving letter, in which he shows what your friendship meant to him.

Allow me to quote a few passages: "You understand that, in the midst of all this, I am thinking of you. More than twenty years ago, ever since Andrzej told me for the first time: 'Duska was in Ravensbrück', I have been aware of the conviction that God gave and assigned me to you, so that in a certain sense I might 'compensate' for what you suffered there. And I thought: she suffered in my place. God spared me that trial, because she was there. Someone might say that this conviction was 'irrational', yet it was always within me—and it continues to remain. Upon this conviction gradually developed the whole awareness of the 'sister'. And this, too, is something that lasts a lifetime. It, too, continues to remain."

From these words it is clear that for John Paul II you remained "Dusia", his little sister, and he was "Brat", your brother. As pope, Karol Wojtyła wanted to confirm all his "old" friendships.

True friendship lasts forever, and therefore after his election to the papacy nothing changed in our relationship.

Were you and your family regular guests of the pope?

We always met whenever I was in Rome. And my family and I spent summer vacations with him in Castel Gandolfo.

As often happens in such circumstances, there were some who accused you of influencing the pope, even in decisions that did not concern your professional field.

Look, Karol Wojtyła and I always used to discuss God and the problems in the world. In short, our conversations dealt with theological and pastoral problems, and there was no reason for gossip.

I brought to Rome the books that I had read, and we discussed them together. Obviously, we spoke also about personal matters, about the family and the children. And he was interested in everything, because he loved people and never spoke ill of anyone.

He admitted to me that as a youth he was terrified by the sentence: "Do not judge and you will not be judged", which left a deep impression on him for the rest of his life.

Is it true that you used to read books to him?

I read books to Karol Wojtyła for more than fifty years.

He had a formidable reading ability: he could read two books at the same time. One with his eyes, the other by listening to another person read.

He loved Polish literature and poetry. The last book I read to John Paul II dealt with the economic situation in Poland between the two wars.

Archbishop Mokrzycki wrote that you were at the Holy Father's side until the end: in the days of his illness and agony.

When John Paul II was admitted to the Gemelli Hospital for the last time, Monsignor Dziwisz arranged for my visits: every day he sent one of the Vatican automobiles to bring me to the hospital.

During the last four days, too, I was able to stay near the pope.

On Wednesday (March 30), I visited him to read him a book. But on Thursday, Dziwisz called me to tell me that the situation had worsened. I arrived at the apartment and did not leave until the end, that is, until midnight on Saturday, April 2.

Before the conclusion of the beatification process of John Paul II, you published a book with forty letters from Karol Wojtyła (published in Italian as Diario di un'amicizia: La famiglia Półtawska e Karol Wojtyła, *by Edizioni San Paolo). This book elicited strong reactions: it was rumored that the publication might complicate the ongoing process. Was it really necessary to make that correspondence public?*

During a meeting on November 14, 1993, in the presence of Archbishop Michalik, the pope asked me to write some memoirs. I began, but there were pressures, and he asked me to stop. But before dying, he told me that I had to give my testimony.

Did John Paul II read the printer's proofs of the book?

The Holy Father read everything. The only thing he did not see was the final chapter.

What happened after the death of John Paul II?

After his death they told me that, as long as I live, I must indeed give my testimony: who could do it in my place, after my death?

So I wrote a draft of the book and submitted it to two Polish archbishops. The first, Archbishop Michalik, after reading it told me: "Publish it!"

After that I showed the diary to my present confessor; in responding to my doubts, he pointed out to me that I do not have exclusive rights to John Paul II, whereas the Christian people, like the common people, have a right to know their saints.

Therefore, I also put the text into the hands of the postulator of the cause of beatification and canonization. Monsignor Oder read everything, confirmed the opinion of the two archbishops who had reviewed the first draft of it, and finally commented that the contents of this book would be enough to support the whole process. Because these letters do not "reveal" me but, rather, Karol Wojtyła. And so the volume was published.

It is not the diary of my life but of my soul. In it are published my letters to my confessor and his replies. In this way I tried to inform the people about another aspect of the personality of this saint, his profound spirituality.

For more than fifty years, you saw Karol Wojtyła close up; could you tell us, what were the major goals of his mission, and were they achieved?

His pastoral priority was to bring man closer to God through love of neighbor. And man learns to love in the setting of marriage and family. John Paul II therefore strove to sanctify the human family, to teach people "the beautiful love" (as he called it) that is generated in marriage and develops in everyday life within the walls of the home.

This is an endless task, so that one cannot say that his goals were achieved. In any case, I hope that, in the future, people will continue to study his teachings and put them into practice.

Often it is asked how John Paul II ever attracted so many people, even people who were away from the Church.

It is simple: he attracted people because he truly loved everyone. And the people understood it, sensed it, and naturally repaid that love with love, affection with affection.

IV

Co-workers in the Vatican

Joaquín Navarro Valls

THE "VOICE" OF JOHN PAUL II

Perhaps not everyone knows that the world-famous journalist Joaquín Navarro Valls (born in Cartagena, Spain, on November 16, 1936), the "spokesman" for Pope John Paul II and therefore considered even far beyond the precincts of the Vatican to be one of the most authoritative figures on his pontificate, graduated *summa cum laude* in medicine and surgery in 1961, thus earning a degree as a specialist at the Universities of Granada and Barcelona, and then continued his studies for a doctorate in psychiatry. Because of this training, Navarro Valls, while not concealing the great sorrow he felt at the time, was a particularly well-qualified witness to communicate in detail to the media and to the world the state of Wojtyła's health in the interminable days preceding his death.

A student of journalism at the University in Pamplona, Navarro—as he is commonly called—later earned in that same field a scholarship to study at Harvard University, graduating in 1968, but completing also a degree in communications in 1980.

After coming in contact with Opus Dei in the fifties, he joined as a numerary member; in the early seventies he moved to the Roman headquarters of the Work, where the founder, Monsignor Josemaría Escrivá, was still living.

A reporter for *Nuestro Tiempo* at first, and then Rome correspondent for the Madrid daily newspaper *ABC*, in this capacity he came into contact with John Paul II, as he followed his apostolic journeys.

After becoming acquainted with him—and, obviously, after "evaluating" him with the utmost discretion—the pope surprisingly decided in 1984 to appoint him director of the Vatican Press Office, a job he even held for about two years after the death of Wojtyła, consenting to the wishes of his successor, Benedict XVI.

A pivotal figure in Vatican communications for more than twenty years, Navarro Valls, who as a representative of the Holy

See also spoke at various international conferences sponsored by the United Nations and was personally acquainted with the high-ranking leaders of the principal religions and heads of state throughout the world, is an extraordinary witness of our time, besides being one of the persons most profoundly connected, even today, to John Paul II.

From October 16, 1978, to April 2, 2005: the twenty-seven years of the pontificate of John Paul II have left their mark on the life of every Catholic of our generation. I wanted to start our conversation by asking: What were you doing on that afternoon in the late seventies?

Of course I was in Rome, following the election of Karol Wojtyła. And trying to understand the significance of that choice in that strange year in which we saw, within a few months, three popes. Everything seemed a bit unreal. And since I had to inform the readers of the newspaper for which I wrote about those facts, I tried to remain at the level of what had happened, with a detached realism that, on the other hand, was not easy to maintain.

Was it expected that an unknown Polish archbishop would give fresh impetus to the papacy, the Church, and the entire world?

He was unknown to the general public but certainly not within the Church or, most importantly, among the cardinal electors.

As a young bishop he had participated in all the sessions of the Second Vatican Council—the only Polish bishop to do so. He had traveled widely. Some of his books were well known in translation. Then came his election. His first words, but also his body language, immediately made clear that a new page had started in the history of the papal institution.

When did you meet him for the first time?

I saw John Paul II up close for the first time the day after the white smoke.

One of my sources informed me that the new pontiff would be going to Gemelli Hospital to visit his friend, Monsignor Deskur.

So I went there directly. Since I was a physician, it was not difficult for me to enter the room of the patient, who at that moment was not conscious.

A little later, Wojtyła arrived at the hospital and was brought to his friend's room.

I found myself with him. He did not speak much in those moments, but his expressive gestures were very eloquent. His youth was evident. His natural spontaneity, also: not one ritual or typical gesture. Everything about him was genuine, normal.

I sensed that anything was possible with this pope: something radically new had happened at the summit of the Church. The future appeared to be wide open in all directions.

When did the first meeting between you take place?

I had accompanied him as a journalist on his first journeys abroad. But the first personal encounter was in his apartment, at dinner. He had summoned me and knew that two years previously I had been elected president of the foreign press in Italy. He immediately proposed the topic of conversation: he wanted suggestions about how to manage the Holy See's communications so as to make clear and incisive its human and Christian message in the public sphere that was by then saturated with messages and information.

I said what at that moment seemed to me to be quite obvious. Some time afterward, to my great surprise, I was informed that the Holy Father had appointed me director of the Press Office of the Holy See.

Naturally I had my doubts, which were neither few nor of little account: the job—at least as I conceived of it—seemed immense. But I trusted him: it was his decision, not mine. And it seemed to me consistent to accept it because of who he was. Even with its risks. And also with the awareness that my life was about to change professionally. Perhaps also humanly.

For more than twenty years you worked for the pope as director of the Vatican Press Office (but everyone recognized you as the "pope's spokesman", which is much more than a head of the Press Office). What were your relations like during that long period?

They were the relations that seemed necessary to carry out that work, with that pope, in a very peculiar age of modernity. Without very frequent personal contact, that work could not have been done. I told him that from the start. And he let me know that that was exactly what he had in mind.

But by accompanying him constantly on his journeys, on his vacations in the mountains, during his stays in the hospital, and in many hours of conversations, I had the opportunity to gain access to his thoughts, to his way of seeing his own ministry and of interpreting the historical time in which he happened to live. And to gain access also somewhat to his personal relationship with God. It was an extraordinary wealth that, over the hours and years that we spent together, developed not only into admiration but also into friendship.

How is it that John Paul II cared so much about relations with the media?

Your question could easily be turned around: How is it that the media cared so much about John Paul II? Because in reality journalists were fascinated with John Paul II and followed him from the beginning of his pontificate.

The reason for this interest, certainly, had to do with his magnificently expressive ways. But also, and perhaps most importantly, because of what he said, because of the contents, the ideas and thoughts that his wonderful expressiveness clothed so well. An ancient message—that of the Gospel—that was manifested in a way that attracted the people's interest.

He knew the contemporary intellectual, cultural, and moral parameters so well that it was not difficult for him to present precisely those human and Christian truths that society and the people needed most. Even many non-Christians felt attracted by that message as never before.

The modern world, which wavers between arrogance and bewilderment, was questioned by a vision that is tremendously human and at the same time completely spiritual. The man of our times—that is, each of us—finally found solid ground on which to begin to understand himself and his proper relationship to God.

Who did Karol Wojtyła become for you?

A pope, of course. But also a person I liked very much from the purely human perspective. Someone from whom I learned much; so much that even I may not be fully aware of it. An exceptional man who also had the generosity to be open to trust, familiarity, and pure affection.

A pope, a father, and a friend at the same time. And even then I saw him as a saint, too, that is, a man who was able to say Yes to everything that God asked of him. And he never asked only a little of him.

Recently you stated that in many things that have been written about John Paul II there is no lack of facts, but what is missing is a true portrait of the man Wojtyła. Then what was he like, this man who became pope?

I would need a lot of space to answer this question. But allow me to say one specific thing that may not be widely known: he was a happy man. He had a very good disposition.

In his outward expression, he smiled readily, but as the years went by, because of the muscular rigidity due to Parkinson's disease, that outward smile eventually disappeared. In contrast, joy always quivered in his heart.

He was not only an emotionally optimistic man; he was truly happy. Whereby happiness was more than an emotional state; for him it was a profound conviction.

This trait seems to me essential to any interpretation of Wojtyła the man.

What did the death of John Paul II mean to you?

The end of his sufferings. The return to God of someone who was madly loved. The moment of infinite joy for him.

I remember that in one press conference during those days, a German journalist asked me: "Do you miss John Paul II now?" I answered, "No." And I tried to explain: "Before, I used to speak with him one or two hours a day, according to the circumstances of our work. Now I can speak with him twenty-four hours a day."

His death opened up a new dimension in my personal relationship with him, which from that moment on could be even more intimate.

What sort of Church did the "Polish pope" leave to us?

A Church with more hope. A Church where to many people God seems to be more of a Father, closer and less enigmatic. A more fearless Church because she trusts more in God. A more generous Church because she has learned that she can give more. A Church where young people not only listen but are also able to make themselves heard and can even teach the grown-ups. A Church that is humbler and at the same time bolder. A Church where there is no lack of problems, yet she is able to identify and name these problems and therefore can find solutions.

You noted the great diplomatic gifts of John Paul II, which allowed him, together with Reagan and Gorbachev, to change the world that had emerged from the Second World War. Could you tell us something in this connection?

By now historians agree that the historical developments that changed the lives of hundreds of millions of persons began in 1979, with the first journey of John Paul II to Poland. Of course it took ten years for the change to be completed, but the process began then.

The last time I met President Mikhail Gorbachev, we remembered the time in 1988 when Cardinal Agostino Casaroli and I brought to him at the Kremlin a long letter from John Paul II. "That was the beginning of everything", he replied. He was right, because for him that was the decisive moment, and his decisions took into account what had happened from 1979 on, the errors of his predecessors, from Brezhnev to Chernenko, and the experience that had accumulated in Poland and in other Warsaw Pact countries.

What had happened then?

In 1981, when the invasion of Poland seemed imminent, John Paul II wrote a letter to Brezhnev, recalling the commitments made by the U.S.S.R. when it signed the Helsinki Final Act.

There was no written reply to that letter, but the invasion—contrary to the predictions of American President Ronald Reagan—did not take place.

Moreover, in those years the Holy Father continued to visit Poland, even under martial law. One word from him, incorrectly interpreted by the people, could have unleashed a popular revolt that, in turn, could have "justified" armed repression.

Those years, from 1979 to 1989, were a masterpiece of prudence and boldness that his wisdom and, most importantly, his prayer kept together in an effective balance.

How did you notice that John Paul II, the man who was leading the Catholic Church and influencing the political world, was also a great mystic?

At certain times I entered the chapel in his apartment without him perceiving that he was not alone. I saw him there, in front of the tabernacle, in conversation with God. And sometimes he began to sing. Not a liturgical chant.

His dialogue with God was continual. He needed to pray continually. Even on public occasions or in front of the crowds. In him, it seemed to me, action and contemplation were one and the same thing.

The last time I saw him outside of the bed where he finished his earthly life, he was on a wheelchair being pushed by a nun. It was a short trajectory: scarcely thirty-three feet between his bedroom and his chapel. Physically, too, he wanted to stay close to the tabernacle. And he stayed there for hours. Those were his final days on this earth.

Immediately after the death of John Paul II, the process of beatification began in order to establish the heroic character of his Christian virtues. What were the virtues that impressed you the most?

He was never capable of wasting a minute; he was never in a hurry. He prayed much, but his prayer was nourished by the needs of others. He was in love with his priesthood. He accepted everything from God, even the most difficult things and those that were the most painful, physically, too.

His incredible boldness was the consequence of his trust in God, not in himself.

He had no need of anything: his poverty was absolute. He liked to read very much, but his reading did not steal one minute of the time that he was obliged to dedicate to his ministry.

He loved confession and went to confession once a week on a set day. When he had to ordain bishops or priests, he fasted the day before.

With what feelings will you participate in the canonization of John Paul II?

With no surprise whatsoever, naturally. But during the ceremony, perhaps I will say to him what I have already said to him several times: "Thank you, John Paul II, for the masterpiece that, by the grace of God and your generosity, you made of your life."

What keeps the former director of the Vatican Press Office busy today?

I have returned to university life. I am president of the Advisory Board of the Biomedical University of Rome. I am also on the Administrative Council of the Enrico Mattei Foundation. I write and, unfortunately, I also have to travel frequently.

Will you publish someday your memoirs of those memorable years?

Maybe I ought to have done so already.

Pawel Ptasznik

"HIS CONSTANT CONCERN?
THE SALVATION OF MANKIND"

Young people felt that they were understood and loved by John Paul II, although he did not make allowances for them; always and tirelessly, he showed them nothing but the narrow, demanding road of the Gospel.

The fruits of his pontificate were truly abundant. Although the experience of the *Papaboys* is famous—a generation of young Italians who gathered spontaneously after rediscovering the faith and enthusiastically coming back to the Church thanks to the inspiring pontificate of Pope Wojtyła—much less well known are the many, many personal stories of young people who, again thanks to John Paul II, discovered their vocation to the priesthood or the consecrated life.

The phenomenon was quite evident in the pope's native country, particularly in the eighties, when there was a genuine vocations boom.

Among the Polish youth fascinated by the figure of Wojtyła the priest was Pawel Ptasznik. Born near Kraków, he was ordained a priest in 1987 and went on to study at the Theological Academy in Kraków and at the Gregorian University in Rome, where in 1995 he earned a doctorate in dogmatic theology. After returning to Poland, he remained there only one year, because in 1996 he was called to the Vatican, to the Polish section of the Secretariat of State, of which he became the head in 2001. In that capacity, he was one of the closest collaborators of John Paul II, during the final phase of his pontificate, among other things taking dictation as the pope composed his speeches, addresses, homilies, and other teachings orally.

Monsignor Ptasznik agreed to share "the great grace and good fortune to live almost ten years in close contact with John Paul II", by reason primarily of his work, while he was also able on various occasions to participate in the papal audiences and journeys as well as many joyous and convivial moments.

Already when John Paul II broke his arm, and later because of his Parkinson's disease, you helped him to compose texts, becoming "the hand" of the pontiff. How was the work organized?

We used to meet in his study. Before working, the pope liked to take a short walk on the terrace of the Apostolic Palace: it helped him to pray and meditate. After joining me, he would greet me, sit down, half-close his eyes, and begin to dictate. Every so often, he asked me to read a passage or an excerpt so as to hear it again; then he continued.

I was always astonished that the texts written in this way needed no revision. Furthermore, John Paul II cited from memory excerpts from the Bible, the Fathers of the Church, and the documents of the Second Vatican Council.

Indeed, it is astonishing to examine the manuscripts of the first encyclicals of John Paul II: they are practically perfect, with very few corrections, as though the pope had in his mind the entire lengthy document even before writing it.

That is true. John Paul II had a phenomenal memory, visual memory, too: for example, he remembered persons whom he had met years before, even for a few short moments.

Returning to the dictated texts, from time to time the pope would stop and ask me: "What do you think about it?" Obviously I felt embarrassed: indeed, in regard to the writings of the pope, who was a great philosopher and theologian, what significance could the opinion of a young priest have? But he did not ask my opinion just for the sake of asking, but, rather, he truly wanted my collaboration. Then I would try to offer him some suggestion.

All the co-workers of John Paul II emphasize the importance he assigned to prayer. Would you like to add anything on this subject?

Prayer was the engine of his existence. John Paul II prayed incessantly, in whatever situation he happened to be. First of all, he was

assiduous in reciting the traditional daily prayers, including the Holy
Rosary, reading the breviary, adoration, and meditation. Moreover,
every Thursday he made a so-called "holy hour" (an hour of Eucharistic adoration) and, on Friday, the Way of the Cross. And since he
did this during his apostolic journeys, too, the organizers had to take
this into account.

The pope prayed also for specific intentions, because he received
a great many requests for intercessory prayers sent by the common
people from all over the world. He had expressly asked us to inform
him about them, and therefore we used to prepare a list of intentions
together with a folder containing the letters. He kept these prayer
requests in his private chapel, on the *prie-dieu*. Once I saw there also a
page from the Polish edition of *L'Osservatore romano* with the organi-
zational chart of the Vatican Curia and with the names of the Polish
officials: I had proof, therefore, that he used to pray for his collaborators, and for me too, and this discovery greatly moved me.

John Paul II used to pray, then, for the whole Church. But not
abstractly: he spoke to us about the "geography of prayer". On his
writing desk, he kept an atlas of the world; every day he leafed
through it and chose a country or a diocese for which to pray. And
after many years of his pontificate, he knew very well both the
strengths and the weaknesses not only of the individual dioceses, but
also of their pastors.

What do you say about the sacramental life of John Paul II?

It is well known that the celebration of the Eucharist was the focal
point of every day. He never omitted it: even when sick and during
his hospital stays, as soon as his condition allowed him to do so, he
would concelebrate from his bed with his secretaries. And so he did
until the end.

He never wanted to say Mass alone. From the first days of his pontificate, he asked that people be invited, so that the Eucharist might
be an ecclesial, communal act. He prepared each time with meditation and prayer. He celebrated with great interior involvement.
He was always recollected, as though immersed in the mystery of
Christ's Passion. Nevertheless, in his way of performing the ceremonies, he always displayed a great peace and serenity, because—as he

used to say—the Eucharist is also the commemoration of the Lord's Resurrection.

On the other hand, not everyone is aware of the fact that John Paul II went to confession regularly, at least once every two weeks. His confessor, Monsignor Stanislaw Michalski, lived at the Polish Church of Saint Stanislaw, where I too resided. Obviously Monsignor never spoke about it, but all of us there could tell that when the car with the license plate "SCV" [*Stato Città Vaticano*, Vatican City State] appeared at the front door—usually on Saturday—it was to bring him to the pope.

I must add, finally, that the Holy Father also spent a lot of time meditating on the Gospel and on tradition. This was not only a spiritual exercise, since he was truly seeking inspiration and the solution to problems in the light of the sacred texts.

Every time the physical condition of Pope Wojtyła worsened, even minimally, the media exploited it to fantasize on his possible resignation. In your opinion, did John Paul II ever actually consider the possibility of resigning?

In fact, when the Holy Father turned eighty in 2000, the problem had presented itself. And he had stated explicitly in his testament: "In the year in which I reach the eightieth year of my life (*octogesima adveniens*), it is necessary to ask whether it is not time to repeat with Simeon from the Bible, *Nunc dimittis* [Lord, now you let your servant go in peace]."

Personally, however, I am convinced that, especially at those moments when illness put him to the test beyond human limits, Karol Wojtyła nevertheless felt completely himself, in spirit and in body, subject to the Lord, so that he wanted to remain utterly faithful to the promise he had given upon accepting the Petrine ministry.

You were close to the pope on April 2, 2005, also. Could you tell us about that day?

On March 30 the last general audience was held. The Holy Father appeared at the window of his apartment, but he was not able to speak. I had the sad honor of lending him my voice and reading his final thanks and greeting to the Poles. On the morning of April 2, the pope blessed the new crowns for the images of the Black Madonna preserved respectively in the Shrine of Jasna Góra in Częstochowa and in the Polish chapel of the Vatican grottos. That was his last public act.

I met John Paul II at noon, when he was still fully conscious. Present also in his room was Cardinal Ratzinger. We prayed together for a few minutes. Then, when the moment came to say goodbye, Monsignor Dziwisz asked the Holy Father to bless me. I knelt down, and he placed his hand on my head and made a sign of the cross. That blessing will remain forever in my memory and in my heart.

His death must have been a dreadful moment.

For me it was less sorrowful than what I experienced several days earlier, immediately after the pope's second return from the Gemelli Polyclinic. It was the end of March; Monsignor Dziwisz called for me and, handing me a bundle of handwritten papers, told me: "It is necessary to begin translating it." It was the Holy Father's testament. While the whole world was praying for his recovery and that he might again lead the Church, I was forced to realize that the day was swiftly approaching on which his last will and testament would be read.

The original text had been composed in Polish, and it was up to me to translate it into Italian. I was struck particularly by the passage that described those days, perhaps very precisely: "I would like once again to entrust myself entirely to the Lord's grace. He Himself will decide when and how I am to end my earthly life and my pastoral ministry. In life and in death [I am] *Totus Tuus* through Mary Immaculate. I hope, in already accepting my death now, that Christ will give me the grace I need for the final passover, that is, [my] Pasch. I also hope that he will make it benefit the important cause I seek to serve: the salvation of mankind, the preservation of the human family and, within it, all nations and peoples (among them, I also specifically address my earthly Homeland), useful for the people that He has specially entrusted to me, for the matter of the Church and for the glory of God Himself."

So the Holy Father had written as early as 1980.

In translating these words, I had before my eyes the crowds of women and men, young and old, who had come to Saint Peter's

Square to pray for the pope but also to demonstrate their faith. I thought: "Precisely in these moments, the desire that John Paul II expressed in his testament is coming true: his death, like his life, is truly useful for the most important cause that he served tirelessly: the salvation of mankind." This cause was his constant concern.

After a few years this pope, who had been inspired by such lofty and noble thoughts of love and service for Christ and the Church, was elevated to the glory of the altars. What, in your opinion, are the outstanding features of the sanctity of John Paul II?

Personally I was always fascinated by his humanity, that is, by his simplicity, kindness, and the attention he paid to every person he met. I always wondered whether this attitude was the foundation of his spirituality or was the result of it. I deduced from this that it was an expression of his personal integrity: his union with God and his total entrusting of himself to Christ were transformed into love for man and confidence in man, into complete harmony between the truths that he proclaimed and his daily life, in his love for creation, in his serenity, and also in his sense of humor.

When you were with John Paul II you felt calm, secure, uplifted, appreciated, worthy, better, capable of aspiring to your own sanctity.

Camillo Ruini

"GOD MADE HIM HIS OWN.
THAT IS, HE WAS A MAN OF GOD"

Cardinal Camillo Ruini (born in Sassuolo on February 19, 1931) was the pope's vicar for the diocese of Rome and archpriest of the papal basilica of Saint John Lateran from July 1, 1991, until June 27, 2008, during the pontificates, first, of John Paul II, who called him to Rome, and, then, of Pope Benedict XVI, who confirmed his appointment until he had completed his seventy-seventh year.

President of the Italian Episcopal Conference (CEI) from March 7, 1991, until that same date in 2007, and president of the Cultural Project of the CEI until January 31, 2013, he was considered for almost thirty years the most influential person in the Church in Italy as well as an incisive interpreter of the political and ecclesiastical situation not only in Italy but in Europe and throughout the world.

1978 was called the year of the "three popes": within a few months sorrowful and important events followed one after the other: the death of Paul VI, the election and the death of John Paul I, and the conclave that led to the choice of John Paul II. What did you feel when you heard the news of the election of the archbishop of Kraków to the papal see?

In 1978, I was a priest in the diocese of Reggio Emilia. On the evening of October 16, I was just returning home. A television was on in the reception area of the rectory, and I heard the news of the election on television. I listened with astonishment. At the beginning I could not even manage to identify who Cardinal Wojtyła was.

But my astonishment was immediately accompanied by a deep satisfaction. For two reasons: first, because the choice of a Polish bishop seemed to me to be very positive and significant; second, because this made a break in the centuries-old tradition whereby it seemed that the pope always had to be Italian.

Then, when I heard the newly elected pontiff speak from the balcony of Saint Peter's Basilica in his Italian, which was a little unsure but very incisive, my heart expanded. I had the impression that we were dealing with a very charming man with a great capacity to bear witness.

When did you have the opportunity to meet John Paul II for the first time, and what impressions did you take away from that encounter?

I met the Holy Father in the autumn of 1984. I was one of the vice presidents of the committee that was preparing the convention of the Italian Church in Loreto, to which the pope attributed great importance. For this reason he wanted to see me, and one evening he invited me to supper.

I was impressed by the attention with which John Paul II listened to me and, at the same time, by the precision with which he asked me questions. I was struck also by the simplicity of the person, the immediacy of the relationship that I established with him. I understood that the pope was deeply acquainted with the situation in our country, and most importantly I shared his convictions about what Italy and the Italian Church needed then.

Your Eminence, you followed the first years of the pontificate of John Paul II from a "diocesan" perspective. Do you recall how this foreign pope was perceived at the beginning by the people?

I sincerely believe that the idea of a "foreign pope" was never a problem for the people: the Italians are not nationalistic, much less chauvinistic.

It is true, however, that there were some who sought to suggest doubts, not so much about the fact that he was a foreigner, but rather about the fact that, coming from a different world, he would not be able to understand our problems. It was also thought that, from the ecclesial perspective, the council had penetrated less in Eastern Europe, behind the Iron Curtain.

But these were ideas that circulated mainly in the newspapers, in addition to some specific ecclesial settings. To most people, the pope gave an impression of confidence and optimism as well as a deeply rooted faith, and that was the essential thing, and the people liked that.

In 1991 the pope called you to Rome to work alongside him in his ministry, as vicar for his diocese, a task that you performed until June 27, 2008. What was Pope Wojtyła's relationship with the Eternal City like?

John Paul II had a great awareness of the importance of Rome and of its universal openness, which corresponds to the universal openness of the pontificate of the bishop of Rome. I cannot forget the many times that he emphasized, even when speaking privately, that he was the "universal pastor", in other words, the pope, by virtue of being bishop of Rome. The title of "bishop of Rome" was the foundation for his universal role. For him, therefore, the relationship with Rome was not something incidental; it was the very root of his pontificate.

The Holy Father deeply loved Rome. Cardinal Dziwisz, in his book *A Life with Karol*, recalls that every evening, before going to sleep, John Paul II used to bless the city. The pope took great care of his ties with the city and the Romans: it is enough to remember his visits to the parishes and the relations he maintained with the priests, the seminary, the intellectuals, the university community, the sick, and the poor.

For many years you were one of the highest-ranking leaders of the Church in Italy, being at the head of the episcopal conference, first as its secretary, then as president. From this perspective, how would you characterize the relations between the pontiff and his country?

With Italy, too, John Paul II had a profound rapport. He was well aware that the bishop of Rome is the primate of Italy and resolved to perform that role in his favorite key of "servant of the servants of God".

In particular, the Holy Father maintained that the Italian Church was not sufficiently conscious of her great riches and potential or of her responsibility. Still significant in this regard is the letter he addressed to the Italian bishops in 1994 on the responsibilities of Catholics in the present hour. The pope concluded that letter by writing that to Italy has been entrusted the great task of preserving and nourishing for Europe the treasure of faith and culture that was transplanted to Rome by the apostles Peter and Paul. He maintained—often citing President Pertini, with whom he had a relationship of true friendship—that the Church in Italy is much more important than ecclesiastics realize. Precisely by virtue of her roots, the Italian Church has a particular responsibility in Europe and in the world.

The detractors of John Paul II described him as the "Polish pope", underscoring his alleged provincialism and nationalism. How do you evaluate Wojtyła's love for his land?

How many times the Holy Father spoke to me about the history of Poland, which he knew very well! In order to understand correctly his feelings for his homeland, it is necessary to refer to everything he said, for example at the United Nations, about the concept of "nation" and of "international society", understood as a "family of nations".

To the pope, a nation was not something self-contained with antagonistic tendencies. It was, instead, a primordial and fundamental fact, especially on the cultural level: a community of culture within which men, families, and civilizations grow. For John Paul II, therefore, the concept of nation was highly positive, even though he was quite conscious of the risks and degenerate forms of nationalism.

But the pope never confused nationalism with the concept of nation and, accordingly, never thought that the concept of nation was outdated and had to be abolished. We know how much John Paul II fought for Europe, but for him Europe could not exclude the nations. And every nation has its role, its characteristics, it physiognomy.

Unfortunately there is a widespread opinion, even in certain ecclesiastical circles, that nations can be an obstacle to the construction of the European Union. Does it not seem to you that John Paul II thought about that Union in a different way?

More and more often the European Union tends to take authority away from the nations, and that is a serious danger. If we seriously want to build Europe, we need to build it on the basis of "subsidiarity", which means that Europe must do only what the individual nations cannot do well by themselves.

It is wrong to try to impose from above "European" standards of social and family life. It is obvious that the Poles, the Spaniards, the Scandinavians, or the English have very different ways of living and thinking. To ignore those differences leads only to useless tensions. Instead, the European Union ought to deal especially with the major themes of the economy, defense, and foreign policy, where it alone can act with adequate effectiveness.

In saying this, I think I am correctly interpreting the thought of John Paul II, which was the fruit and at the same time at the origin of his way of being, acting, and living. Indeed, his love for Poland did not prevent him from loving humanity. If there is a man who truly did much for the whole world and particularly for the poor countries, that man is Karol Wojtyła.

Let us speak now about the man. What sort of a person was Karol Wojtyła; what were his human relations with his closest collaborators like?

He knew how to listen and loved to listen. He would intervene mostly to summarize and to make decisive choices: he was very firm when he made decisions that he considered to be just for the Church and for the preservation of the faith.

But, I repeat, in his relations with individual persons he was very respectful, trustful, and amiable. I never saw the pope treat anyone in a negative way, and I often envied his ability to listen to people so patiently and calmly. He never watched the clock: in this, too, he proved to be a free man.

Your Eminence, you described John Paul II as a "man of God". Would you explain for us exactly what this means?

We can say that someone is a "man of God" if God is that man's master, if the Lord has "taken possession" of him and made him his own. Karol Wojtyła was a "man of God" because God was at the center of his life. It is very significant that the pope pointed to Holy Mass as the fulcrum of his day, every day. This tells us about his relationship with God.

Then, on the level of major international events, it was impressive how he always interpreted history from the divine perspective (think, for example, of his encyclical *Centesimus annus*). But he also adopted this perspective in more immediate and everyday matters. Therefore prayer and action were closely connected in him: he was a man who lived in the sight of God and acted while always seeking to discern his will.

I realize that speaking about the heritage of a great pope who led the Church for almost twenty-seven years is very difficult, but could you try anyway? What did the pontificate of John Paul II mean for the Church and for the world?

It meant many things. We all remember the contribution he made to the fall of the Iron Curtain. But fundamentally important also is what he did to restore trust to the Church and to her mission and to vindicate the dignity and the rights of poor people; and also everything he did to protect the rights of unborn children.

But if we want to look deeper and find the key to his pontificate, we must turn to his relationship with God and the way in which he translated it in terms of his pastoral activity and its impact on historical events.

He had one basic conviction: secularization is not a fatal, irreversible fact; the world and history are not necessarily getting farther and farther away from the Creator. When I met him, in 1984, he was already convinced that the world, somehow, was turning a new leaf, that the high tide of secularization was already behind us. This basic conviction was certainly part of his cry: "Do not be afraid!"

Friends who die always leave an empty space. What do you miss about John Paul II?

I miss a lot. I offered him my modest service for more than twenty years. There was affection for him, there was also a familiarity with Father Stanislaw: I could not always disturb the Holy Father, and therefore I often spoke with his secretary. One never becomes resigned to the absence of a person who is loved and esteemed.

In another respect, however, in a deeper sense, I do not feel his absence: I pray every day to John Paul II and feel united with him in the certainty that he is continuing, even more intensely, what he did in the years during which he was in Rome with us.

Karol Wojtyła was proclaimed Blessed on May 1, 2011, and will be proclaimed a saint on April 27, 2014: What significance do these events have for the Church and for you personally?

Long before he died, John Paul II had won the hearts not only of Catholics but of a great many persons of every faith and nationality. His funeral showed the world how much he was loved, and this sentiment has remained very much alive over the course of these eight years, from 2005 to 2013. His beatification and now his canonization, which are being accomplished in a very short time, are the official, solemn validation of the popular intuition that was expressed as early as the evening of his death, in the acclamation "Santo subito!" (A saint immediately!)

These events, therefore, have a tremendous significance for the Church but also for humanity. They present to everyone his life and his death, his relationship with God, his giving of himself to his brethren, his apostolic and missionary dedication, and his acceptance of suffering as a great model of faith in action.

For me personally, these are days of profound joy, because of the affection that binds me to him, because of my gratitude to him, because of my gratitude to the Lord who gave me the grace to be very close to a saint for twenty years. I had the honor of opening and concluding the diocesan phase of his cause for beatification and canonization; today I thank God that I can be present at the definitive conclusion of the whole process.

Angelo Sodano

"AS THOUGH SEEING HIM WHO IS INVISIBLE"

The cardinal who receives me in audience in his apartment within the Ethiopian College, at the heart of the Vatican Gardens, is one of the most prestigious figures of the Church of Rome. Today His Eminence Angelo Sodano (Piedmontese, born in 1927 on the island of Asti) is dean of the college of cardinals; in contrast, from 1988 until 2005 he was one of the closest collaborators of John Paul II, first as "secretary for relations with states", then as "secretary of state" (offices that, with some oversimplification, are compared to those of the "foreign minister" and "prime minister" of the Holy See).

It could be said, without fear of misrepresentation, that Cardinal Sodano together with Cardinal Joseph Ratzinger and Cardinal Camillo Ruini were the "pillars" of the Roman Curia during Wojtyła's pontificate.

This career diplomat, despite his advancing years (which he does not show), has lost none of his brilliant intelligence, keen judgment, or calm determination. He is very reluctant to grant interviews—thus observing one of the chief requirements of true diplomats—but on the occasion of the canonization of John Paul II, he consented to make an exception.

Your Eminence, for a long time, even as a priest in the Secretariat of State, you worked on relations with the then-Soviet Union, with Hungary during the imprisonment of Cardinal József Mindszenty, with the Rumania of Ceausescu, and in general with all the countries of Communist Europe. Did you expect then that in 1978 the new pope would come from one of those countries?

Yes, that is right: from 1968 to 1977, I collaborated in the Secretariat of State together with the late Archbishop Agostino Casaroli (who was later created cardinal by Pope John Paul II). It was a time of great zeal for the peoples of Central and Eastern Europe.

Those were the years of the pontificate of the Servant of God Pope Paul VI, who felt that it was a compelling duty to help the bishops, the Christians, and all people of goodwill in Eastern Europe to profess their own faith freely. I remember very well that historical period, of which Cardinal Casaroli, before his death, gave an overview in his fine book *The Martyrdom of Patience*.

Already at that time I had become acquainted with the vitality of the Polish Church, the courage of her pastors, and the fearless strength of the faithful. And already at that time the great figure of the archbishop of Kraków was well known among the cardinals of the Curia.

I, too, had become acquainted with Cardinal Wojtyła. It happened here, in the Vatican: I was introduced one day by the late Cardinal Jean Marie Villot, who at that time was secretary of state. Bishop Wladyslaw Rubin, at that time secretary general of the synod of bishops, and Monsignor Andrzej Maria Deskur, secretary of the Commission for Social Communications, also spoke to me about him with admiration. (Both of them, later on, received the purple hat from Pope John Paul II.)

For these reasons, the election of the archbishop of Kraków to the See of Peter was not a surprise to me.

What did the choice of a Polish pope mean for the Church?

For the newspapers and the television networks of that time, it might have been a novelty. But for anyone who knew the two-thousand-year history of the Church, his election could not cause any surprise.

Therefore, actually, it fit in perfectly with the tradition of the Roman pontificate and was a new invitation to reconsider it as a whole. In every age and in every specific historical transition, the Holy Spirit has in fact raised up the Successor of Peter who best corresponds to the needs of the Church.

Thus the cardinals assembled for the second conclave in 1978, after praying for a long time to the Holy Spirit and invoking his light, saw that it was opportune to ask their confrere, the archbishop of Kraków, to be willing to perform this special service to the Universal

Church. And he, trusting in the help of the Lord and in the maternal protection of Mary Most Holy, accepted that urgent request. And that is how the Church gained that great pope, whom today we venerate at the altars.

At the beginning of the pontificate of John Paul II, you were apostolic nuncio in Chile and had to confront two major problems: the international crisis that erupted between Argentina and Chile with regard to sovereignty over the Beagle Channel and the political situation in that country, which was led by a military government. How did you manage to deal with two such sensitive cases?

Indeed, shortly after my arrival in Chile, in November 1978, I had to endeavor, on behalf of the Holy Father, to promote peace between Chile and Argentina.

The territorial dispute between the two neighboring countries was caused by a century-old quarrel over sovereignty in the southern zone, between the Atlantic and the Pacific. It was certainly a real problem, which was then complicated by the nationalist campaign that developed in both countries. The danger of armed conflict was imminent. So it was that, before Christmas 1978, the new Pope John Paul II immediately sent, first to Buenos Aires and then to Santiago (Chile), one of his extraordinary representatives, Cardinal Antonio Samoré, who, in collaboration with the nuncios of the two countries, began the patient work of mediating between the respective governments.

It was a peacemaking process that avoided a fratricidal war and led the parties to sign a "Treaty of Peace and Friendship", which ensured a fruitful era of collaboration between those two sister nations.

With the military government of Chile, then, I again pursued a line of dialogue, according to the instructions of the Holy Father. Finally, I had the joy of preparing for the visit of John Paul II to Chile in 1987. It was a journey completely devoted to the theme of reconciliation. The motto of the late pontiff was: "El amor es más fuerte", love is stronger than political divisions and social conflicts.

The facts later proved him right. His visit effectively contributed to the pacification of the nation, and our saintly pope has been remembered there every since as the great apostle of peace.

The pope must have held you in great esteem if in 1988 he called you back to the Vatican to entrust to you the office of his "foreign minister" and, later on, secretary of state. In that way you became his closest collaborator: the head of the Roman Curia, which assisted the supreme pontiff in his mission. Could you tell us what was John Paul II's method of governing?

In the fifteen years in which I was John Paul II's secretary of state, I always admired his great pastoral balance. It was a marvelous synthesis of tradition and modernity, in light of the teaching of Jesus, who in a well-known parable praised the man who could draw from his treasury "what is old and what is new", *nova et vetera*, according to the beautiful Latin text of the Gospel of Saint Matthew (13:52).

And it was a method of governing that was always inspired by the principles of Christ's Gospel, always guided by the higher light of faith.

I would like to emphasize that for this reason, too, he was acknowledged as a saint, and we can contemplate him in glory: not only because of the sanctity of his personal life, but also because of the sublime spirituality that guided him in his pastoral decisions.

In a short time, John Paul II also became a great world leader. Did this fact influence the work of the Holy See's diplomacy?

Certainly John Paul II always emphasized and appreciated the Holy See's presence in the life of nations and in international organizations.

And during the twenty-six years of his pontificate, that presence was greatly strengthened in the international field. Through the renewed work of the "papal representations" scattered throughout the world, the Roman pontiff can effectively help promote the spiritual progress of peoples, defend their rights of religious liberty, and foster peaceful international coexistence.

Many observers and scholars, but also common people, wondered how such a mystical pope managed to influence the fate of the world. Your Eminence, how would you answer that question?

I answer that these are the surprises of the Holy Spirit, who always enlivens his Holy Church. Returning to the discussion started earlier in reference to the election of a Polish pope, I wish to emphasize that anyone who starts to study Church history will notice that, in the most difficult moments, the Holy Spirit has always raised up men and women of faith who were capable of making a deep mark on the society of their time. So it happened also with the life and works of John Paul II.

This is the actualization of what we profess in the Nicene Creed, which speaks to us about the Holy Spirit who is the "Lord and giver of life". And that same saintly pope of ours reminded us about this in one of his fourteen famous encyclicals, *Dominum et vivificantem*, written in 1986 in preparation for the Great Jubilee Year 2000.

With this vision of faith, John Paul II desired to lead us into the Third Christian Millennium, precisely because he went forward with a supernatural vision of human history. And we can say about the pope what the author of the Letter to the Hebrews attributed to Moses, describing him as the one who advanced toward the Promised Land "as [though] seeing him who is invisible" (Heb 11:27). That is how John Paul II saw and journeyed toward eternity.

V

Taking Care of the Pope

Egildo Biocca

"ON TOUR" WITH THE POPE

In 1978, Egildo Biocca was working in the Vatican Vigilance Corps (*Corpo di Vigilanza*, the name then for the gendarmerie of the Holy See). As a Vatican policeman, he saw Paul VI die that year and witnessed the election of John Paul I and his unexpected departure. Lastly, on October 16, he saw a third pontiff appear for the first time on the balcony of Saint Peter's. And it was a historic event, perhaps even more so than the alternation of three popes in such a short time: after five centuries, the cardinals, in fact, had elected a non-Italian cardinal.

The first thing that impressed him about John Paul II was his strong voice; after the plaintive voice of Giovanni Montini and the bashful way in which Albino Luciani spoke, the words of the new Successor of Peter sounded powerful and reflected his physical strength, also.

Over the course of several days, it was discovered that John Paul II was an athletic man who loved the mountains and skiing. Then Biocca really started to like the pope, because having been born in the mountains, near the Gran Sasso in central Italy, he, too, was a skier and a great hiker. (It was no accident that he performed his military service in the Alps.)

Because of his knowledge of the mountains, his physical strength, and his talents as a skier, Biocca became one of the organizers of Pope Wojtyła's private tours and his regular traveling companion.

Today he is retired and with great nostalgia relates the facts about these papal "escapades".

When did you become involved in organizing the private trips of John Paul II?

The first two excursions were the only ones in which I did not participate, because as soon as our commander, Camillo Cibin, noticed that well-trained individuals were needed for this type of outing to the mountains, he turned to me.

From then on, I was involved in organizing all the private trips of the Holy Father.

How was an excursion of the pope organized?

My boss used to send me in advance to scout the areas that had been selected. Then I would write a report in which I indicated the places where, in my opinion, we could bring the pope.

After that, we would repeat the on-site investigation with Cibin. The commander was very demanding and tried to choose spots where there would be no passersby, but that was not always possible.

Lastly, Father Stanislaw called me to ask me where we were going. I always described several possibilities to him, but he, having the utmost respect for our evaluations, always ended by letting us choose the destination.

Did the excursions take place during the vacations, when the pope was based at Castel Gandolfo, or at other times, too?

They happened throughout the year, departing from the Vatican, also. The preferred days were Tuesday and Thursday.

It is said that you considered only itineraries and places in the Abruzzo region.

We often went to the mountains in Abruzzo, because you could get there quickly on the expressway, but we also took trips to Tuscany and to the seashore.

To the seashore?

Of course, we brought the Holy Father there, also: to Passoscuro, not far from Rome, to the coast near Civitavecchia, to Porto Santo Stefano on Monte Argentario.

Did the Holy Father walk on the beach?

The pope used to walk on the beach only at the resort in Passoscuro, which is located in an extraterritorial zone.

In other places, we used to identify reefs along the coast from which he could admire the sea and breathe the fresh air.

How did you travel?

We used our private automobiles, with Italian license plates. The Italian police did the same, and the police escorts were in civilian clothes.

How long did these drives last?

Although he arose very early, the pope always had a few items of business to dispatch, and so, generally, we would leave in the late morning.

As soon as we arrived in the mountains, we started to hike or to ski: in the early years, the Holy Father used to walk a lot. Punctually at noon, John Paul II would stop, even when he was skiing, to recite the Angelus.

At around 1:30 or 2:00 P.M. we would eat outdoors: often we had nothing but rolls. As the years went by, we used more equipment: we used to bring two tents, one for cooking, the other at the disposal of the Holy Father to allow him to rest and take shelter from the wind or the rain. We brought a chair as well, always the same one, which had become his favorite.

We, his traveling companions, did the cooking, and we competed with each other in offering him the most authentic, traditional specialties. After dinner there was coffee, and then the pope retired. Very often, before returning to the Vatican, we used to light a bonfire and sing the Alpine songs he liked so much.

Who participated in these outings?

Besides the Holy Father, there was naturally Father Stanislaw and, then, Angelo Gugel (the majordomo of John Paul II), and often

Father Styczen; in later years, Sister Tobiana used to come, too. Then there were three or four of us from security: Massimo Illuminati, Valentino Binci, Nunzio Bracchi, and I.

How did the pope dress when he went on an excursion?

When he went skiing, he wore the appropriate clothing: a very ordinary suit of a nondescript color with a woolen zucchetto. At first he used his old skis and climbing boots. Later on, people gave him more modern equipment as gifts.

On the other hand, when we took long walks in the mountains, the pope used to wear a conventional hiking outfit. At least he did early on; as the years went by, he preferred to wear white clothing, obviously with climbing boots on his feet or at least athletic walking shoes.

You, the members of his security team, did everything possible to avoid meetings with "strangers". But were you always successful?

Of course not, it was just not possible. Every so often we would meet persons along our way, and we had to try to manage the situation as best we could.

Could you reveal to us how these encounters went?

I could tell you so many stories. One day, as we were walking through meadows, I saw a shepherd with his flock. I hurried to meet him and started to speak with him: I asked him a few questions, as though I were interested in buying some sheep. He was so taken up by our conversation that he did not notice the party that had passed right by him.

Another time we found ourselves at the Marian shrine in Mentorella. While John Paul II was praying in the church, a woman and her son came in. Father Stanislaw did not dare to prevent people from entering and walking around just because the Holy Father was there. And so those two persons came in and greeted the pope. As they were going away, I heard the boy saying to his *mamma*: "We can't tell them that we saw John Paul II in Mentorella, because no one would believe us, or else they would think we were crazy."

Tell another story.

During one of our walks in the Aosta Valley, they informed me that along our path there was a small group of mountain climbers, members of the CAI [Club Alpino Italiano] from Teramo. I went over to them and told them that we were soldiers, that we were doing some experiments. After that I told them to change their route. And so we avoided an encounter.

But Father Stanislaw always recommended that we should not cause anyone trouble; and every time it happened that someone appeared unexpectedly, he gave him the opportunity to meet the Holy Father.

Did the excursions of the pontiff change in the final years of his life?

When the pope no longer hiked, we used to choose very scenic places, where he would sit. In any case, until the end, he always made an effort to take a few steps, to walk a bit.

There was one incident that I have told no one. In the winter of 1997 or 1998 (I do not remember exactly, but walking already used to tire him greatly), I gave the pope a surprise: without telling him ahead of time, I brought him a pair of skis for a trip on the snow. When we were already standing on the snow, Father Stanislaw showed them to him. Then he put them on his feet and skied beside me for two or three hundred yards; that was the last time he skied!

John Paul II liked very much to ski: on the slopes I used to see him content and happy.

What sort of "traveling companion" was John Paul II?

First of all, I would like to stress that we gendarmes were very discreet and did everything possible so as not to disturb the pope. For him, those excursions were not just a time of recreation and relaxation, because they offered him a special opportunity to pray, to talk with God, to admire nature and all creation.

I must then admit that, personally, I always was a bit in awe of the Holy Father, although I was so close to him for many years: I was dealing with an extremely charismatic man, whereas I am shy by nature.

That being said, he always proved to be a really tremendous traveling companion, because he was able to spread cheer and to put everyone at ease.

And he was also an understanding man. Once, while mountain climbing, I stepped on one of his hands. No one noticed anything because the pope said nothing but just looked at me as though eager to reassure me: "Nothing serious happened; you do not have to apologize."

Can you estimate how many private excursions John Paul II made?

Many more than a hundred.

Renato Buzzonetti

THE HEROIC PATIENCE
OF THE POPE AS A PATIENT

From the time he appeared on Saint Peter's Square with his round, smiling face and boundless energy, walking at his dynamic pace on the long flight of steps of the *piazza* and carrying his crosier as though it were a twig, they used to call him "God's athlete". It seemed that that powerful, indefatigable man would never need physicians, but all that changed one fine spring day in 1981: the bullets fired by the assassin's hand did not kill him, but they seriously undermined his iron constitution.

From then on, John Paul II became also a "man of sorrows": sickness and suffering entered his life overbearingly, and the Gemelli Polyclinic Hospital was a place well known to the pope and frequented by him. He jokingly took to calling it "Vatican III".

From this experience was born the apostolic letter *Salvifici doloris* on the Christian meaning of suffering, but also a new dicastery dedicated to the sick and to health care workers: with the motu proprio *Dolentium hominum*, John Paul II in fact created the Council for Pastoral Assistance to Health Care Workers. Finally, we owe to Pope Wojtyła the World Days of the Sick, on the feast day of Our Lady of Lourdes, February 11.

Little by little, Parkinson's disease and osteoarticular problems immobilized him, making him a prisoner in his own body, but the pope continued his mission without hiding his ailments: not because he was an exhibitionist, but in order to vindicate the value and role of every person in society, even of those who are sick or disabled.

The last weeks of his life marked his Calvary: the pope who had always taught us how to live in those days showed us how to confront death.

Alongside John Paul II, until he drew his final breath, was his personal physician, Doctor Renato Buzzonetti, a truly special witness of the life of the "pope of suffering".

Doctor, you have gone down in history as the physician—or, more precisely, the head physician—of three popes. Could you tell us what is the job of the personal physician of the pontiff?

The personal physician of the pope is entrusted with the task of watching over his state of health and helping in the prevention and treatment of illnesses with which the pope may be stricken. To the extent possible, he should follow him in the various phases of his activity, especially in those that involve the risk of compromising his health or of unforeseen trauma associated with the events, even insignificant ones, connected with a normal routine, or else with traumatic incidents. In this very delicate service, the physician makes use of the efficient operating system of the Directorate of Health Services of the Governorate of the Vatican City State and, when away from Rome, the collaboration of the local medical authorities.

When did you meet John Paul II for the first time?

I met him in the *Sala regia* (state hall), a few minutes after his first solemn blessing from the central balcony of the Vatican basilica.

I was the physician for the conclave and headed the team dedicated to health care assistance. Shortly before that, I had been worried upon seeing the new pope leave the Sistine Chapel. His brand-new white zucchetto seemed to "float" over the group of purple-robed prelates and monsignors who joyfully surrounded him. He stood in the *Sala regia* for a few minutes to greet the members of the conclave. Someone surely informed the new pope about my long friendship with then-Monsignor Deskur, who had been admitted to the Gemelli Polyclinic Hospital in very serious condition. When he came over to me, John Paul II put a hand on my shoulder, asked for news of his great friend, and requested that I keep him informed about the latest developments in his illness, but the telephones were disconnected because of the conclave. He insisted: "Get the information yourself."

On that day I could not foresee that on December 29 of that same year I would be called in directly by the Holy Father and invited to be his personal physician.

Indeed, in 1965 I had joined the medical corps of the Vatican Governorate with a part-time professional job, while at the same time serving as a hospital physician in one of the largest and most efficient public health care systems in Rome and in all Italy. But I did not know Karol Wojtyła even by sight.

Who proposed that you become the personal physician of the new pontiff?

In the afternoon of December 29, 1978, while I was at work in San Camillo Hospital, I unexpectedly received a phone call from then-second secretary of the pope, Monsignor John Magee, who asked me to stop by. That evening I arrived at the papal apartment, assuming that the monsignor had a touch of the flu.

I was led into a little room, and, shortly thereafter, to my great surprise, John Paul II appeared, accompanied by two Polish physicians. He had us sit around a table and told me in still-unsure Italian that he wanted to appoint me his personal physician. Then he began to describe for me his case history very exactly, with dates and numbers, although at that time Karol Wojtyła was a person in good health.

That evening he invited me to supper. The next day I wrote to his secretary, Father Stanislaw, telling him that I accepted and that I was ready to resign whenever the Holy Father wanted me to; in the same letter I added that I would be criticized for having accepted such an important job and that the pope, in turn, would be criticized for having chosen me. And both things proved to be precisely true in the following years.

From then on, you were at the side of John Paul II for more than twenty-six years, following him everywhere, even on his travels throughout the world. How were your relations?

They were characterized by great simplicity.

For my part, there was always a filial and respectful sincerity; on the pope's part, an affectionate trust that was manifested very soberly in gestures, words, and with evident benevolence.

How did the pope behave as a patient?

Karol Wojtyła was a docile, attentive patient who wanted to know the cause of his minor or serious ailments, yet without the irritable but understandable curiosity of many sick people.

He was very precise in pointing out the symptoms from which he was suffering. He did this because he was determined to get better so as to return to work as soon as possible and, even before that, so as to be able to pray in his chapel: that was the attitude he maintained until the end.

John Paul II never displayed moments of discouragement in the presence of suffering, which he always confronted with courage and conscious acceptance. Like any patient, he was not fond of injections, but he put up with them, hoping for a cure.

Karol Wojtyła was a very healthy person, brimming with energy, and he seemed to have no need of physicians. That all changed with the assassination attempt. What can you tell us about that terrible incident?

The chronology of May 13, 1981, has already been recounted a thousand times, from every angle. To this day, however, the direct testimony of the victim has been missing, which we can try to reconstruct just from a few fragments of what he experienced during those tragic hours.

In the ambulance, in which I accompanied him to the Gemelli Polyclinic Hospital, he ceaselessly pronounced these words in Polish: "Jesus ... my Mother ...", and nothing else. In the text of the Angelus message, which he laboriously read from his bed in the intensive care unit the following Sunday, he added on his own initiative the word "brother" when he pardoned the assassin. Perhaps that is the eloquent summary of those hours of struggling to survive.

For my part, I never asked the pope anything about those truly terrible days. He spoke of them a few times with me, half-smiling: "That man wanted to find out the third secret of Fatima by force", he said, alluding to Ali Agca.

I can recall, however, that, at the Gemelli, as he awoke from the anesthesia after the surgery, which lasted five hours, he commented: "Like Bachelet." Then I objected: "No, Your Holiness, because you are alive and are going to live, but Bachelet is not."

I think he mentioned that name because the assassination of Judge Bachelet the year before had left a deep impression on him. That was the vice president of the Superior Council of Magistrates, who was killed by the Red Brigades in 1980. The pope knew him well because, as ex-president of Catholic Action in Italy, he was a member of the Pontifical Council for the Laity, in which Cardinal Wojtyła had participated. And he decided to celebrate a Solemn Mass in Saint Peter's for the repose of the soul of Vittorio Bachelet a few days after his death.

And the time came when the pope fell ill with Parkinson's disease.

The first symptoms of Parkinson's were noted by me around 1991.

Thinking back to that time, I think there was no precise moment at which the pope discovered he was suffering from that disease. For a long time he subjectively underestimated some troubles, and only later did he begin to ask for explanations about the tremor.

I told him that the tremor is the most obvious symptom of that neurological disease but that the tremor in itself never killed anyone, although it is a serious impediment. Very soon, however, additional balance problems developed that made the situation precarious.

In the following years, the life of John Paul II was further complicated by painful osteoarticular symptoms, particularly serious in the right knee, which prevented him from remaining on his feet for a long time and from walking easily.

These two sets of symptoms compounded and complicated each other, the Parkinson's disease and the osteoarticular problems. Therefore the use of a cane became necessary, and then devices such as specially fitted chairs and the moving platform.

How did the pope endure the pains and infirmities that limited his movements and freedom?

His physical pain, in the final stages, was intense, but it was not the only reason for his suffering. He suffered above all because of the state of helplessness in which the disease had confined him. It was a moral, spiritual suffering, which deeply affected him: the suffering of a man who was impeded, of someone who had lost his physical autonomy and was confined to bed or to an armchair. The suffering of a man on the cross, who nevertheless accepted everything with courage and patience: he never asked for sedatives, not even in the final phase.

At a certain point he could no longer do anything by himself, and for him the long, trying days of total physical helplessness had come: John Paul II was unable to walk or speak, except with a hoarse, weak voice; his breathing had become labored, interrupted, and he ate with increasing difficulty.

How distant, now, were the days of the memorable World Youth Days, the major speeches to global assemblies, the fearless climbs in the Dolomite Mountains or the vacations on the ski slopes, and the exhausting pastoral visits to the parishes of Kraków and Rome.

When the hour of the cross came, he was able to embrace it without hesitation. "Vexilla Regis prodeunt" [from a Latin Holy Week hymn beginning "The standards of the King go forth"]: having recognized the insignia of the King, the pope submitted, once again, to the will of Christ.

Do you recall some particularly dramatic moment?

I have already said that John Paul II did not surrender to suffering. But I could stress one particular moment tinged with amazement and anguish: immediately after the tracheotomy in March 2005, when he awoke from the anesthesia, although he had given his consent previously, he only then realized that he could no longer speak. Unexpectedly he had to confront that extremely burdensome reality. He asked Sister Tobiana for a little slate, on which he wrote in an unsure hand in Polish: "What have you done to me.... *Totus tuus.*"

That was his realization that he had been brutally thrown into a new existential condition, which was immediately lifted up by his act of entrusting himself to Mary.

Sometimes the newspapers and television repeated strange stories about the so-called escapes of the pope from the Vatican. Can you tell us something about this?

Certainly, because when these "escapes" occurred, I was present.

In the first years of the pontificate, his favorite trips were to mountainous or maritime localities not far from Rome, which involved long walks or else many hours of skiing. As the Holy Father advanced in years, the distances on foot gradually became shorter and the excursions, after a speedy trip by car, concluded with a long stay in the shade of a tent that was set up in front of a serene panorama, facing the horizon of the sea or at the foot of mountaintops that were often still covered with snow.

The bag lunch was a time for quiet conviviality with his traveling companions. Toward sunset, before setting out on the road back to Rome, the pope enjoyed listening to mountain songs sung by his little entourage, and the Vatican gendarmes and the Italian police escort used to join in. It was up to me to direct that impromptu chorus as he watched with amusement.

Do you remember details of these "escapades"?

I remember well one outing to the mountains, near Arcinazzo, in May 2003. John Paul II was suffering at that time from functional disability because of his right knee, which caused him very intense pain. After asking me for clarifications about the state of his health, the pope took the opportunity to tell me that I would have to remain his physician "forever". Obviously I did not forget that day.

Nor can I forget the last summer vacation in the Aosta Valley, in July 2004, when in Prat Sec, not far from Courmayeur, on a green meadow and under the blazing sun, I found the courage to communicate for the umpteenth time to Monsignor Dziwisz my proposal to resign, after twenty-six years of service. But he saw my bid and raised me: he said that I must not and could not, because that was the will of the Holy Father, and he confided that the pope remembered me every day in his Holy Mass. I had to surrender.

Karol Wojtyła was your patient, but for you, a believing Catholic, he was also the head of Christendom, the Supreme Pastor. How did you perceive the spirituality of the pontiff?

Pope Wojtyła lived in an intimate union with the Lord, made up of ceaseless contemplation and prayer. He had a faith of steel and a soul that resonated with Polish romanticism and Slavic mysticism.

He was a person with a penetrating intellect, an ability to synthesize and make decisions quickly, a very strong memory, and, above all, an evangelical ability to love, share, and forgive.

You, together with his personal secretaries and the sisters who looked after him, were one of the very few to have assisted the Holy Father in the terminal stage of his illness. What do you recall of those dramatic days?

Those days left a deep impression on my life; they were dominated by a very serious professional duty, by a painful participation in the human and religious drama that was playing out before my eyes, by a great deal of stress because of the heavy responsibilities that weighed on my shoulders, and, finally, by ceaseless prayer in communion with the pope who was suffering on his mystical cross.

Here are the essential records of those critical moments, which are still quite vivid in my memory and in my heart:

—Thursday, March 31, 2005, at around 11:00 A.M., while celebrating Holy Mass in his private chapel, the Holy Father is convulsed by a bout of shivering, followed by a spike in temperature and a very serious septic shock. Thanks to the skill of the emergency room staff on duty, the critical situation is once again brought under control.

—At around 5:00 P.M., Holy Mass at the foot of the pope's bed as he emerges from the shock. It is celebrated by Cardinal Marian Jaworski with Father Stanislaw, Father Mietek, and Monsignor Rylko. The Holy Father has his eyes half-closed. The cardinal of Lviv administers to him the Anointing of the Sick. At the consecration, the pope weakly lifts his right arm twice, for the bread and for the wine. He gestures as though to strike his breast with his right hand at the moment of the *Agnus Dei*.

—After the Mass, at the invitation of Father Stanislaw, those present kiss the Holy Father's hand. He calls the sisters by name and then adds: "For the last time." His physician, before kissing the venerated hand, says aloud: "Holy Father, we wish you well, and we are all close to you with all our heart."

—After that, since it is Thursday, the Holy Father wants to celebrate an hour of Eucharistic adoration: a reading, recitation of psalms, hymns provided by Sister Tobiana.

—Friday, April 1, 2005, after Holy Mass that he concelebrated, the Holy Father at 8:00 A.M. asks to make the Way of the Cross (he follows the fourteen stations by making the sign of the cross over himself), joins in reciting the third hour of the Divine Office, and at around 8:30 A.M. asks to hear the reading of passages from Sacred Scripture, read by Father Tadeusz Styczen. The medical attendance continues without stopping.

—Saturday, April 2, Holy Mass is celebrated at the foot of the Holy Father's bed; he participates in it attentively. At the end, John Paul II, in mumbled words that are almost unintelligible, asks for the reading from the Gospel of Saint John, and Father Styczen devoutly completes nine chapters of it. As a contemplative man, with the help of those present, he recites the prayers of the day as far as the Office of Readings of the Sunday that will soon begin.

—At around 3:30 P.M., the Holy Father whispers to Sister Tobiana: "Let me go to see the Lord" in Polish. Father Stanislaw relates these words to me just a few minutes later.

Is that precisely what he said?

These words were his "consummatum est" (Jn 19:30). They were not a surrender to the disease or an escape from suffering; rather, they expressed a profound awareness of a *via crucis* that—accepted courageously to the point of divesting himself of every earthly thing and of life itself— was now approaching the finish line: the encounter with God.

John Paul II did not want to put off that appointment for which he had waited since the earliest days of his youth. That was what he had lived for. Therefore, these were words of expectation and hope, of a renewed and definitive commendation of himself into the Father's hands.

During those same hours I, and the other colleagues present, had to note that the disease was progressing inexorably toward the final phase of its course. We had waged our battle patiently, humbly, and prudently, but it had been extremely difficult, because we were all now inwardly convinced that it would end in defeat. The technical know-how and the wisdom of the physicians, the enlightened affection of the members of the household were constantly guided by a total and merciful respect for the suffering man. There was no so-called therapeutic obstinacy; no heroic measures were taken.

Could you continue with the chronology of what happened on the afternoon and evening of April 2 in the pope's room with the whole world outside, in anxious, sorrowful expectation?

—After 4:00 P.M., the Holy Father becomes sleepy and gradually loses consciousness.

—Toward 7:00 P.M. he enters into a deep coma and then into agony. The monitor registers the progressive fading of his vital signs.

—At 8:00 P.M. Mass begins, celebrated at the foot of the bed of the dying pontiff. Monsignor Dziwisz concelebrates with Cardinal Jaworski, Father Mietek, and Monsignor Rylko. Polish hymns blend with those that waft in from the crowds on Saint Peter's Square. A little candle burns on the small table beside the bed.

—At 9:37 P.M. the Holy Father dies. After a few minutes of aston-ished sorrow, the *Te Deum* is intoned in Polish, and from the square, suddenly, people see the window of the pope's bedroom lit up.

You were a helpless witness of the agony and death of the Vicar of Christ. The doctor had to become the Cyrenian.

For the Christian physician, who is often an unappreciated, exhausted, silent Cyrenian, the agony of a man is the icon of the Lord's. Every man has his wounds, wears his crown of thorns, stammers his last words, abandons himself into the hands of someone who uncon-sciously renews the gesture of Mary, of the holy women, of Joseph of Arimathea.

The death of John Paul II involved me even more. It was the death of a man now deprived of everything, who had experienced the hours of the battle and of glory and who was appearing in his interior nakedness, poor and alone, at the encounter with his Lord, to whom he was about to hand back the keys of the Kingdom. In that hour of sorrow and astonishment, I had the sense of being on the shores of the Lake of Tiberias. All of history seemed to be reset back to zero, while Christ was preparing to call the new Peter. The isoelectric line of the electrocardiogram registered the end of the great earthly adventure of a man who was already being called "the Great" and a saint by the people of God, but it seemed to delineate a new horizon, open toward a future that had already started.

John Paul II was able to forge a special relationship with the world of the sick, with the reality of suffering: he was the one who announced that the World Day of the Sick would be observed on the same day as the feast of Our Lady of Lourdes; he was the one who wrote the apostolic letter Salvifici doloris *on the Christian meaning of suffering; he was the one who sought contact with the sick during all his audiences and all his journeys; he himself was a pilgrim to Lourdes. Did the Holy Father discuss these topics with you, Doctor?*

Pope Wojtyła was a very reserved man, not much inclined to confide intimate matters. But his attitudes and gestures spoke to people with plain, unmistakable eloquence.

His relationship to the world of the sick and of physical, mental, and spiritual suffering was a hallmark of the almost twenty-seven years of his pontificate. He proclaimed the "gospel of suffering", first of all embodying it himself, becoming a credible and authentic witness of the proclamation of salvation, of which he was the providential herald at the sunset of the twentieth century.

The twenty-sixth anniversary of *Salvifici doloris* was celebrated on February 11, 2010. It was an amazing page in papal teaching, which still today is like a surprising commentary on the sorrowful life experience of John Paul II.

From this perspective, I maintain that the most sublime moment in his public testimony to the gospel of suffering was the pilgrimage of John Paul II to Lourdes, which he made on August 14–15, 2004. It was, significantly, the last of his 104 international journeys.

What in particular struck you on that occasion?

The pope was suffering, seriously hampered in his movements and gestures, compelled to interrupt the reading of his invocation to Mary in front of the grotto of Massabielle, but he did not retreat, he did not shirk his duty as a son and a pastor. A sick man among the sick, he was determined to participate in the traditional ceremonies of that great Marian shrine.

He did not hide his helplessness as a sick man; he had no conventional inhibitions; with the simplicity of a just man, he declared his fidelity to life, that gift of God that had to be lived out to the very end, without evasions and without shortcuts.

This was a great catechesis that celebrated illness that is accepted in imitation of the Crucified, not as a humiliation and condemnation, but as a gift of grace and a sublime hymn to human life, and thus becomes a sign of contradiction and of hope.

Arturo Mari

"I HAVE PHOTOGRAPHED SIX POPES.
HE CONSIDERED ME A SON"

John Paul II treated him like a son and did not conceal these paternal feelings toward his photographer. During the journey to the
United States, in Saint Louis, Arturo Mari found himself in the parlor
together with the pope and President Clinton to shoot some photos.
At a certain point, the pontiff turned to the president: "Do you know
who he is?" "No", Clinton replied. Then the pope said: "This is
Arturo", and afterward added: "Arturo is like a son to me."

But who is Arturo Mari? Ever since I have lived in Rome, that is,
since 1980, this sturdy man with the round, smiling face, in his black
suit, white shirt, and dark, polka-dotted tie, was part of my Vatican
"scenery". There was no public appearance, audience, or Holy Mass
of the pope at which you would not see Arturo with his two or three
cameras on shoulder straps. And so it was for fifty-one years, without
a single day when he took off or called in sick!

With just one exception: On April 29, 2007, Arturo for the first
time attended a papal ceremony merely as a spectator. He was sitting
in the first row of Saint Peter's Basilica as an invited guest, together
with his wife, an Ecuadorian from Guayaquil: Pope Benedict XVI
was ordaining twenty-two new priests, and among them was Juan
Carlos of the Legionaries of Christ, Mari's son.

Then Arturo resumed his work, until his well-deserved retirement.
In the meantime, his face became so well known and recognizable
that a witticism used to make the rounds in Rome: "Who is that man
dressed in white beside Arturo Mari?"

I met the photographer in a bar on the Borgo Pio, in the district
where he was born in 1940. Mari is, as they say in these parts, a
"romano de Roma", a "Roman from Rome". Indeed, to be more
precise, he is a *borghiciano*, a citizen of the Borgo district: the ancient
quarter of the capital where during the Middle Ages many, many

Saxons, Franks, and Longobards on pilgrimage stayed; in their language, they called it the *burg*; mispronounced in Italian, it became *borgo*. Here, the streets too are called *borghi*.

Even though he has traveled so much, Arturo's whole life was nourished here, in these *borghi* in the shadow of the dome of Saint Peter's, where he lives to this day. Here was born also his long adventure with cameras, and thanks to this passion he became the photographer of the popes.

In the autumn of 1978, when John Paul II was elected, Arturo did not imagine that this "foreign" pope would become "his" pope [*Pápa*], becoming also something of a dad [*papà*] to him. From that day on, he served him with filial devotion for twenty-seven long years of his pontificate, "writing" in images the extraordinary history of it.

Our conversation started, however, with his memories of the beginning of his career in photography.

How did you become passionately interested in photography?

My father was an amateur photographer, and, in order to keep me from wasting time wandering the streets, he placed me in the photography lab of a school in the district. At the age of six, I already knew everything about photography. To make a long story short, I was a sort of "photographic" child prodigy. Since my father worked in the Vatican, like my grandfather, incidentally, everyone there, too, knew about this passion of mine.

When I was sixteen years old, the editor-in-chief of *L'Osservatore romano*, Count Giuseppe Dalla Torre, was impressed by some of my pictures and wanted to become acquainted with me.

I went to the newspaper for the interview scheduled for eleven o'clock in the morning on March 9, 1956, and was accepted as a photojournalist and joined the Giordani Company, because at that time *L'Osservatore* had no photographic service.

My job was to follow the pope, and I continued to do so for a good fifty-one years.

In short, you began during the reign of Pius XII. What do you remember about your first day of work?

My first assignment was a beatification ceremony in Saint Peter's, with Pope Pacelli presiding.

At that time, public ceremonies with the pontiff were extremely rare and lasted a long time. When I saw Pius XII, a tall, long-limbed figure, wearing the tiara and seated on the *sedia gestatoria* (portable throne), I became very emotional.

But what was I to do? There were photos to shoot. I lost no time and never stopped doing it.

What was Pius XII like?

He was a great, very dignified man. I have never forgotten how one day, as he entered Saint Peter's Basilica, he stretched out his arms, as in the photograph taken of him in the San Lorenzo district after it was bombarded by the Allies: he made a broad, solemn, protective gesture.

Those were different times. The pope was just emerging from the dreadful experiences of the war. He almost never left the Vatican, and when in 1957 he went to inaugurate the new Vatican Radio center in Santa Maria di Galeria, not far from Rome, it seemed to everyone that he was going to the other side of the world.

Pacelli was the first of the six popes you immortalized; the last was Benedict XVI. What would you like to tell us about Pope Ratzinger?

That he is a man full of tact and sensitivity. He is a great worker: despite his age, as pope he never rested, apart from an occasional walk in the garden or the time to recite the Rosary. His table was always buried in papers.

I think that nobody truly realizes how much the pontiffs work. All problems are going to end up on their desk.

They say that Benedict XVI was a bit impatient in the presence of cameras.

Let's not exaggerate. With me he always proved to be patient and tolerant. When he saw me, just after he was elected, he patted me on the hand, as though to reassure me.

I will tell you a significant story. One afternoon, when the pope was on vacation in the mountains, I told him, "Your Holiness, popes never go on vacation, and here Arturo is the one playing the tyrant, and he would like to take a picture of you to give to the people." No problem: he allowed me to shoot photos while he was walking, writing at his desk, and reciting the Rosary. Then I tossed out the idea: "Of course every so often you play the piano ..." And he, in reply, smiled at me, took off his Fisherman's ring and started to play for me.

Going back to the beginning: after Pius XII, it was the turn of John XXIII, now a saint, together with John Paul II.

Pope Roncalli immediately proved to be different from the others who had preceded him: affectionate, cordial, close to the people. But behind the affability of his manners, he was stern, unyielding on fundamental questions.

During his reign, the pope started to go out of the Vatican more: John XXIII inaugurated the visits to the parishes of Rome; he went to the Bambin Gesù Children's Hospital, then to the Regina Coeli prison, and finally traveled to Assisi and Loreto (I documented the first trip taken by the pope on a train). And what can you say about the announcement of the council in Saint Paul's Basilica?

And with Paul VI you traveled even more.

That is true. In 1964 with Pope Montini, we were in Jerusalem. It was the first journey of a pope by air. We landed in Amman, Jordan. What a thrill to be with the Holy Father in the Holy Land!

In 1970, we flew as far as East Asia and Australia. He was a timid, shy man. It was probably because of his character that the people understood him so little, even though he accomplished so much.

The pontificate of John Paul I lasted a heartbeat in the two-thousand-year history of the Church. But you did your job, the same as always, in time to shoot a few very rare portraits of him.

Yes, I was the only one who took official photographs. I also took pictures that later became famous that depict him in the Vatican Gardens. One of them, in particular, has acquired symbolic value: Pope

Luciani, taken from the back, while he walks along the avenue lined with pine trees. A very melancholy moment, almost a premonition of his tragic future.

Continuing down the list of popes, we arrive at John Paul II.

Twenty-seven years with John Paul II are a separate story. For me he was a true father. When you are with a person that way from six in the morning until evening, it cannot be otherwise. You become one of the family.

In the apartment, the door was never closed to me: it could happen that I found myself facing him unexpectedly or was present at delicate moments, even right in the middle of a discussion, because in a family there are times when they discuss things.

That's just it: because of the pope's kindness, I felt like one of the family. When for such a long time you find that every day you are always half a meter away from a person, you can't help becoming a sharer in his soul. What I experienced at his side I will never forget.

You experienced dramatic moments with him, too. What do you remember about May 13, 1981?

The moments of the assassination attempt in '81 were truly dreadful. I felt ill, but instinctively I took some pictures. Those are photos that I would never have wanted to take.

And what is the photo that you consider the most important?

Without the slightest doubt the shot of the last Holy Thursday of John Paul II.

The Holy Father was following the Stations of the Cross on television, immersed in his thoughts. At the Fourteenth Station, he made a sign. Father Stanislaw asked him what he wanted. The pope wanted the crucifix; for a little while he looked at Jesus, then pressed the cross to his heart, leaning his head against it.

I shot the photo and, for me, that image contained the whole life of John Paul II, all his dedication to the suffering Christ.

Allow me to ask a curious question. Do you know how many photos you took of "your" six popes in those fifty-one years? Somewhere in the millions?

I do not know exactly, but certainly that many.

I recall that when John Paul II went for the first time to Argentina, I shot 600 rolls of film (at that time digital cameras did not exist). While we were there the rolls of film ran out and the apostolic nuncio had to buy me another 200.

More than 25,000 photos for one journey. Not bad at all.

Once I sent a digital camera to tech support to upgrade the firmware. I did not know that inside the camera there was a counter. The technicians called me to ask whether this was a joke, because they had never seen such a high number of shots.

Didn't you get tired of taking what seemed to be the same photos in oft-recurring situations?

In order to obtain good results in my line of work, it is necessary to work with the heart and to reach an understanding with the person being photographed, that is, with the pope.

Popes are not difficult subjects to photograph, but you have to perceive and understand the person as he is. That is the secret. If I had not worked that way, by taking pictures of the same ceremonies that are always repeated, I would have achieved only insignificant shots.

We all experienced also the sad moments of the departure of "our" pope.

I still have before my eyes the final moments of Pope Wojtyła. Six hours before he died, Father Stanislaw called me. I went up to the apartment, came into the room and knelt down.

It was traumatic to see him again stretched out on that bed. He had his head turned away, but when the secretary told him, "Your Holiness, Arturo is here", he turned toward me and, smiling, whispered to me: "Arturo, my heartfelt thanks for everything."

There was something special in his look. He was preparing for another encounter.

It must have been tremendously painful for you.

Yes, it certainly was. But I think that the pope had called me, not just to say goodbye and to say "Thanks" to me, but also, like a good father, to help me to endure his death better.

With his serene eyes he was trying to tell me that he was not afraid, that for him the feast day of his encounter with the Lord was approaching.

Do you miss John Paul II?

It would be silly to say "no". Even though I still think about him as a living person.

Sometimes, when I close my eyes, I get the impression that I see him or hear his voice. Therefore I am convinced that John Paul II is somehow still among us.

"Your" pope is recognized as a saint. What are your feelings as you prepare for the canonization?

The Church has her procedures to declare someone a Blessed or a saint. But I was always convinced of the sanctity of John Paul II even when he was living among us.

I had the great grace of knowing him up close.

VI

Witnesses

Tarcisio Bertone

"A GUIDE, SUPPORT,
AND EXAMPLE FOR EVERYONE"

He met Karol Wojtyła for the first time in long-ago 1964 as a student at the Ateneo Salesiano in Rome: during the Second Vatican Council the superiors of the college wanted to introduce some Council Fathers to the students. One day three Poles were invited, too: Cardinal Stefan Wyszynski, primate of Poland, together with Salesian Archbishop Antoni Baraniak, archbishop of Poznan, and Karol Wojtyła, archbishop of Kraków.

He met the last-mentioned prelate once again in 1976, when Father Tarcisio went to meet now-Cardinal Wojtyła at Fiumicino Airport: he had to bring him to the Salesian University to discuss several questions related to the activity of the religious institute in Poland.

En route he spoke with the prelate about the situation in his country. His cousin, Gianni Bertone, was a journalist and often traveled in Poland, and therefore Bertone was rather well acquainted with the local situation under the Communist regime.

He knew very well, for example, that the cardinal of Kraków—"a man of profound faith, great courage, and brilliant intellect"—was very highly and widely esteemed among Polish Catholics. But he just could not imagine that two years later he would see that man with whom he was now conversing appear on the balcony of Saint Peter's Basilica in papal vestments. Nor could he imagine that he would become one of his collaborators: first as consultor of the Congregation for the Doctrine of the Faith, then as secretary of that same dicastery, and remaining in contact with the Polish pope even when he became archbishop, first of Vercelli and, later, of Genoa.

Our conversation started with his memory of October 16, 1978.

Your Eminence, what was your experience of the day when Pope Wojtyła was elected?

Allow me to say something else first: the premature death of John Paul I caused tremendous sorrow in everyone. And therefore the second conclave in that year commenced in an atmosphere of mourning, bewilderment, and anxiety.

On October 16, when news of the white smoke arrived, I was at the Salesian University in Rome, in Monte Sacro. I jumped into an automobile with my confreres, and in a very short time we reached Saint Peter's Square.

The announcement of the election of Cardinal Wojtyła was very moving for me. The people around us, too, who at first were incredulous and perplexed, understood that such a special choice as this was of historic importance and was the precursor of a new hope. That evening a breath of fresh air wafted through the Church.

In those years you were teaching, among other courses, "Relations between the Church and the Political Community". Therefore I would like to ask you: How did people regard a pope who came from a country behind the Iron Curtain and who, as a priest and then as an archbishop, had had to confront the totalitarian Communist ideology?

Obviously John Paul II was classified as an anti-Communist. He was anti-Communist because he was against any totalitarian, oppressive ideology whatsoever. But at the same time, he was extremely sensitive to social problems, particularly to problems of labor: as early as 1981, he published the social encyclical *Laborem exercens*. Being critical of a certain type of capitalism as well, he proposed to the world the social doctrine of the Church, the "third way".

Unfortunately, after the fall of the Berlin Wall, the situation in the countries of the formerly Communist bloc did not have as positive an outcome as was hoped, and the Holy Father did not fail, in some of his speeches, to manifest his disappointment and to incite his listeners to remain faithful to Christian values in their personal, social, and political life.

Could you tell us something about your work in the Vatican during the pontificate of John Paul II?

I started my formal collaboration with the Curia in early 1979. My first job was to prepare the documentation that would be forwarded to the pope for his address to the Roman Rota.

Next, for several years, I collaborated in the revision of the *Code of Canon Law*. As everyone knows, John Paul II was not a canon lawyer, and therefore he attentively studied those problems that were new to him, by becoming informed and also by organizing a series of meetings.

These circumstances offered me the opportunity to meet the Holy Father. Several times I was invited also to working dinners. I was very impressed by the pope's stamina; he truly appeared to be an indefatigable man. After the morning routine and a working dinner—which ended at 3:00 in the afternoon—I used to return home exhausted, whereas he kept going with other tasks.

What changed with your appointment as secretary of the Congregation for the Doctrine of the Faith?

My relations with John Paul II became "official", because one of the regularly scheduled audiences on Friday afternoon was the secretary's duty. Actually, these meetings became even more frequent, because then-Cardinal Ratzinger, who was the prefect of the congregation, brought me with him or sent me to see the pope on various other occasions.

What memories do you have of those meetings? What was Karol Wojtyła like in private?

He was extraordinarily affable. Once in a while, after I bowed and kissed his hand, he, smiling, would respond with a bow and a sign of reverence. He was very attentive to the presentation and sometimes asked for my personal opinions of one theologian or another, about ecclesial and civil events, thus showing his trust in his interlocutor.

In later years, the invitation to dinner became frequent, with a more familiar exchange and with the participation of Monsignor Dziwisz.

In that period, the Congregation for the Doctrine of the Faith had to deal with many very delicate topics. It is enough to mention the problem of pedophilia that had exploded then in the United States, the third secret of Fatima, the case of Archbishop Milingo, the disciplinary questions concerning some theologians.

That is true. Our dicastery had to deal with many topics, but I want to recall specifically several that I discussed with the pope in depth: christological and ecclesiological questions. John Paul II was worried about the "reductionist" tendencies in Christology and therefore was very anxious to reaffirm that Christ alone is the one, universal Savior of the world. So he decided that the document *Dominus Iesus* should be published in the solemn setting of the Holy Year of 2000. Then he strenuously defended it in the well-known Angelus message on October 1 of that same year.

Concerning the Milingo case, he took a clear stance but at the same time one of great mercy, receiving him personally in audience more than once.

The Salesians, sons of Don Bosco, are very devoted to our Lady. And John Paul II was a Marian pope.

Everyone immediately understood his very deep devotion because of the papal coat of arms that he chose, which features the letter "M" for Mary; and also because of his motto *Totus Tuus*, taken from the writings of Saint Louis Marie Grignion de Montfort.

His love for Mary had its roots in his family and in Poland—as a son of that country, he was obviously devoted to Our Lady of Częstochowa—and he confirmed it as pontiff: it is enough to recall the encyclical *Redemptoris Mater* dedicated to the Most Blessed Virgin or the Marian Year, which he proclaimed in 1987 and the many pilgrimages he made to shrines of the Mother of God.

And we cannot forget the very close "ties" that bound the Polish pope to Our Lady of Fatima.

When speaking about the Marian devotion of John Paul II, you cannot fail to mention the assassination attempt that he experienced on May 13, 1981, on the day of the Feast of Our Lady of Fatima. The Holy Father was convinced that he survived thanks to Mary's protection, because, as he himself asserted publicly, "one hand fired, and another hand guided the bullet so that it would not kill." And that hand was the maternal hand of Our Lady of Fatima.

I think that from that moment on, the features of the pope's devotion changed, too; he began to perceive the Mother of God more and more as "the Lady of History", the "Woman of the Apocalypse" who watches over the fortunes of mankind and of the Church, as well as over his own personal destiny.

In 2002, you left Rome to settle as chief pastor, first in the diocese of Vercelli and, then, several years later, in the archdiocese of Genoa. In that capacity did you continue to meet with John Paul II?

As archbishop of Genoa, I was received rather often by the pope, also while accompanying groups of pilgrims. Every time he saw me, he would say, "I am sorry you went so far away." But I used to reply, "You were the one, Holy Father, who appointed me archbishop of Genoa!"

He repeated that remark to me in January 2005 also, when I saw the pontiff for the last time. I remember that he sang with us the hymn "Madonna della Guardia".

In April of that year, with sorrow, you had to return to the Vatican to participate in the funeral of the pontiff. On that occasion you were able to observe personally the tribute of affection offered to Pope Wojtyła by all the Christian people and the banners with which they declared him: "Santo subito!" Why did the common folk immediately perceive the sanctity of John Paul II?

Besides the immediate impression made by the pope personally, I think there are at least four special reasons that communicated his virtue: Karol Wojtyła appeared as what he truly was, a man of God, a man of intense prayer (sometimes during long meetings he counted the beads of his Rosary); he was an apostle of the nations, a tireless preacher of the Gospel; he was an ardent witness to and defender of the faith; finally, during his long illness, he gave evidence of sacrificing himself for the Church and for humanity, becoming a support and an example for all suffering people in the world.

Your Eminence, you were a collaborator of John Paul II and, when called back to Rome, the secretary of state of Benedict XVI. Could you tell us what distinguished the two pontiffs in their character, in their methods of working and making decisions? And what, on the other hand, did they have in common?

I have wonderful memories of my work alongside Cardinal Ratzinger, who then became Pope Benedict XVI, and alongside Pope John Paul II.

About John Paul II, I recall the forcefulness of his proclamation, of his testimony about the centrality of Christ in human history and especially in the history of the Church, and his passionate love for our Savior.

At the same time, I remember the meekness and the clarity of doctrine of Cardinal Ratzinger. I recall the complete trust that John Paul II had in him, not only because of the official role that he had assigned to him as prefect of the Congregation for the Doctrine of the Faith, but also because of his profound esteem for him personally. He liked to be with him frequently (they spoke German together), and he called him to his bedside before dying to tell him once again, as well as he could, thank you.

Several times I have been asked whether there are character traits that the two popes have in common. Certainly there are. Both lived through the preconciliar experience, that is, the preparation for the great reform of the Church, and participated in the Second Vatican Council. I would say, therefore, that their first common heritage is precisely the Second Vatican Council, with the constant endeavor subsequently to implement the guidelines that emerged from it in the life of the Church in relation to the modern world.

But there is another interesting aspect. Despite the fact that Ratzinger and Wojtyła were sons of different nations and received very different educations, they both went through the horror of totalitarianism and experienced deeply and personally the problems of oppression and of the suppression of freedoms. Yet that did not discourage them: instead, it turned them into two men of God who were passionately committed to the truth and to freedom, lovers of humanity, and therefore friends of every man, champions of the freedom and dignity of the person.

My experience at the side of these two popes, in different capacities, was a school of life, a school of faith, a school of spirituality.

To what extent was John Paul II present in the pontificate of Benedict XVI?

Pope Benedict XVI recalled many times the acts and the teachings of John Paul II, pointing out, especially to the pastors of the Church, his virtues and his example to be imitated. Then he was the one to beatify his predecessor in the memorable ceremony on May 1, 2011.

And on that occasion, I had the honor and the joy of celebrating the Mass of Thanksgiving on Saint Peter's Square the following day.

Javier Echevarría

SANCTIFYING EVERYDAY LIFE

On October 6, 2002, Saint Peter's Square began to fill up at the first rays of dawn. When John Paul II made his entrance, there were more than four hundred thousand people in front of the basilica and down along the via della Conciliazione. That crowd had come to Rome to pay homage to the Spanish priest who, in distant 1928, had founded Opus Dei: a new entity in the Catholic Church, aimed at promoting holiness and the lay apostolate through the "sanctification of work". Seventy-four years later, on that crowded square and in the adjacent streets, the solemn words of John Paul II resounded: "In honor of the Blessed and Undivided Trinity ... we declare and define Blessed Josemaría Escrivá de Balaguer to be a Saint, and We inscribe his name in the catalogue of the Saints, ordaining that, throughout the universal Church, he be devoutly honored among the Saints."

The canonization of Escrivá was an extremely important moment for the Work, because it put an end to a period of its history that was marked by misunderstandings, detractions, and calumnies, which were also reflected in the first unpleasant science-fiction book by Dan Brown. However, all the greatest saints and institutes that adorn the Church have always had to pass through a trial.

But John Paul II regarded Opus Dei and its founder with great confidence and affection.

Not everyone knows that the ties between Karol Wojtyła and this ecclesial reality were constant and intense and that they began long before the election of the archbishop of Kraków to the papal see. Here to tell us about these relations is Bishop Javier Echevarría, the current prelate of the Work, who had the privilege of being very close to John Paul II during his whole pontificate.

Your Excellency, could you tell us when the relations between Karol Wojtyła and Opus Dei began?

During the Second Vatican Council, Father Álvaro del Portillo [who from 1974 to 1995 would be the first successor of Josemaría Escrivá as head of Opus Dei—ED.] was introduced to Archbishop Wojtyła.

After that, there were no other contacts until 1971, when the young cardinal of Kraków, during a synod of bishops in Rome, participated in a conference hosted by Cardinal Höffner and organized by CRIS [Centro romano d'incontri sacerdotali, Roman Center for Priestly Meetings] and promoted by several priests of the Work. On that occasion, they asked him for an interview on the priesthood for a CRIS publication, because it was interesting to hear the voice of a bishop who was working under Communist tyranny. He jotted down the questions and, after a few weeks, sent thirty-one handwritten pages in Polish.

Another time, in 1974, CRIS invited him to be a speaker for a series of meetings on "The Exaltation of Man and Christian Wisdom". The topic discussed by the archbishop of Kraków was "Evangelization and the Interior Man". It was a truly profound speech, with a final reference to an expression with which Monsignor Escrivá identified what he considered the way to build up the peace of Christ on earth: "Sanctify your work, sanctify yourself in your work, and sanctify with your work."

Four years later, Cardinal Wojtyła paid a visit to Don Álvaro in Villa Tevere, the central headquarters of Opus Dei. It was a very friendly meeting.

After dinner we went to the oratory to visit the Blessed Sacrament. The cardinal used a wooden *prie-dieu* that we preserve there as a relic, because it was used by Pius VII and, later, by Saint Pius X. And by Saint Josemaría, of course, to whom the nephews of Pope Sarto had given it as a gift.

No sooner did Don Álvaro inform him about these details than Cardinal Wojtyła immediately got up from the *prie-dieu* to kneel on the floor, but not before having kissed the relic. It was a spontaneous gesture of humility that I have not forgotten.

Wojtyła was very fond of Don Álvaro, and the relationship between them was strengthened after his election to the Chair of

Peter. Holy persons understand one another immediately and get along well together.

Well, then, when was the first time you met John Paul II as pope?

It might seem impossible, but the first encounter took place on the day after the election, on October 17, 1978.

Bishop Andrzej Maria Deskur (then president of the Pontifical Council for Social Communications, later a cardinal), who was very close to Don Álvaro and at the same time a friend of Karol Wojtyła since their seminary days, had been admitted to the Gemelli Polyclinic Hospital because of a stroke.

On October 16, after the election of John Paul II, Don Álvaro telephoned him. He was hesitant to mention the good news, because he was afraid of arousing too strong an emotion that might hurt him. He limited himself to asking: "Andrea, do you know whom they elected?" But Deskur replied vigorously: "They could not have made a better choice." And he added: "If you come tomorrow, you will meet him."

Don Álvaro thought that the sick man was delirious: How would a pope who had just been elected be able to leave the Vatican?

On the 17th, Don Álvaro visited his friend, however. And what a surprise, just outside the patient's room, when they told us that we would have to wait in a corner, together with other persons, because the pope had arrived and the exit on that floor was momentarily blocked off. But my surprise was even greater when, upon leaving the patient's room, John Paul II turned to Don Álvaro and embraced him. Don Álvaro was profoundly moved, and as he filially kissed the pontiff's ring he noticed that he was holding a Rosary in his hand.

That was the first of many, many meetings, because after that I had the opportunity to see the new pope more frequently than we could have imagined.

Do you remember also the first "official" audience?

A few days after that moving encounter in the Gemelli Hospital: on October 28, John Paul II received him for the first time in an informal audience.

On that occasion, Don Álvaro commented that—due to the vacant see, because of the unexpected death of the revered John Paul I—it had not been possible to write the letter that the Holy Father intended to send for the fiftieth anniversary of the founding of Opus Dei. Then John Paul II said, "Then I'll write it!"

Pope Wojtyła was very anxious to give Opus Dei a canonical framework. And in a few years the Work was erected as a "personal prelature". How did you arrive at that very important milestone?

Paul VI and John Paul I had already expressed the desire to bring to completion the legal journey of the Work, but the Lord called them to himself before they could address the question definitively.

John Paul II decided to take an interest in it from the beginning. He placed the matter in the hands of Cardinal Sebastiano Baggio, prefect of the Congregation for Bishops, and a joint commission was appointed, made up of canon law experts from the Holy See and from Opus Dei. The Holy Father attentively followed all the steps and knew the particulars very well.

The technical, canonical details are well known. Here I would like to highlight the paternal concern that the pope showed during the whole process, yet without overriding or influencing the canonists, who worked with complete freedom of research and interpretation in addressing every question.

Not all the bishops were in agreement with the creation of this new "entity" in the Church.

That is true, but the pope proved again to be very careful, prudent, and paternal in addressing the difficulties caused by the objections of several bishops, which were absolutely understandable in dealing with a new canonical scenario. He himself took responsibility for these objections and made arrangements for considering and resolving them adequately.

We mentioned certain criticisms of Opus Dei, but not even John Paul II was spared these attacks. Did you have a chance to talk with the pope about those obstacles?

The Holy Father knew how to take up his cross, but at the same time he was very determined and went forward, seeking the good of the Church.

I will tell you a revealing anecdote: once Don Álvaro participated in the recitation of the Rosary with the pope. John Paul II always prayed with other persons, and, on that occasion, Mother Teresa of Calcutta was present, too. At the end of the prayer, the pope introduced Don Álvaro to her, and she thanked him very warmly for the aid offered to her sisters by the priests of the Work in various parts of the world. Then John Paul II asked her, half-seriously and half-facetiously, "Mother, why do they criticize the pope and Opus Dei while everyone speaks well of Mother Teresa?" And she replied, with great sincerity: "Pray for me, that I may be humble."

You emphasized that John Paul II followed Opus Dei closely. Does this mean that he gave you instructions or that he intervened in the government of the Work?

His most important intervention was, obviously, the erection of Opus Dei as a personal prelature, the act by which he placed this part of the Church, made up of laymen and priests, men and women of every class and social condition, under the jurisdiction of a prelate so that—together with its priests, also—it might better serve the Universal Church, in communion with the particular Churches.

Besides that, the pope suggested to the prelate several apostolic initiatives, since he was quite convinced of the efficacy of the personal apostolate of every member of the Work.

From this perspective, John Paul II promoted with great conviction the international seminary *Sedes Sapientiae*, in Rome, with the objective of forming priests who could become formators in the seminaries of various countries, with particular consideration for those nations that had just acquired freedom after the period of Soviet domination.

For a "new evangelization".

And not just in the East. In 1981, if not before, John Paul was speaking about a "new evangelization", but in 1985, during the synod of bishops, he set this pastoral priority in motion, above all in the countries of Eastern Europe and North America, where the symptoms of secularism were growing at an alarming rate.

Don Álvaro seconded this program, and, as early as December 25 of that same year, he wrote a pastoral letter to the faithful of the prelature, urging them to collaborate in every way possible with this task, which was especially necessary in the countries of old Europe, in the United States, and in Canada.

In this way my predecessor obeyed the pope promptly, and he, in turn, never left us without his support. John Paul II, indeed, continued to encourage Don Álvaro, and later on me also, until the end of his life, to persist in the mission of evangelizing, while fully respecting the proper spirit of the Work. Don Álvaro left that audience greatly reassured, with the renewed awareness of the need always to do the *opus Dei*, the work of God—as he had seen Saint Josemaría do—living in full unity with the Successor of Peter and with all the bishops.

The greatest gifts of John Paul II to Opus Dei were the beatification and the canonization of Josemaría Escrivá.

The Holy Father was very happy to elevate the founder of the Work to the glory of the altars. There were again some misunderstandings before the beatification, the thrashing of the devil's tail, but everything was resolved gloriously.

At the conclusion of the beatification ceremony, John Paul II expressed great joy over having witnessed that multitude in recollection and prayer, and, turning to Don Álvaro, who was accompanying him toward Saint Peter's Basilica, he said: "Now I understand why some sectarians did not want this demonstration of faith to take place."

He added that he thanked the Lord for the ceremony in which he had beatified the Canossian nun, Mother Bakhita, which had allowed him to inform the whole world about the tragic situation of the Church in Sudan. In short, what has remained, for the history books, is the good that devotion to Saint Josemaría is doing throughout the Church. And the pope was aware of this.

During the canonization later on, John Paul II described Saint Josemaría as "the saint of ordinary life", fully in harmony with his idea of evangelizing society through the everyday life of the domestic church, which every family is, in work, in sports, and in social relations.

John Paul II was a person who knew how to listen to everyone. Did he also listen to the suggestions made to him by Opus Dei?

On certain occasions, the Holy Father asked for advice. For example, at the end of 1978, when he inquired whether it was opportune to undertake the journey to Mexico for the meeting of CELAM [the Latin American Episcopal Council]. The region was in a rather delicate situation, and the pope wanted to know Don Álvaro's opinion. He turned to him in the presence of other persons and had already heard various opinions on the subject. Don Álvaro simply suggested that he make the journey, because it would be a great good for the Church in Mexico, in Latin America, and throughout the world. Of course, the Holy Father later consulted also with others and with the dicasteries of the Roman Curia. But the journey was made, with the results that everyone knows.

At various times Don Álvaro suggested, then, that the pope should write a letter or an exhortation about Saint Joseph, in order to promote devotion to him among the faithful and to ask him to protect the Church, just as he had protected the Holy Family of Nazareth. I remember how extraordinary his joy was when, on August 15, 1989, John Paul II published the apostolic exhortation *Redemptoris Custos*.

It is said also that some members of Opus Dei had something to do with the mosaic of our Lady, Mater Ecclesiae *(Mother of the Church), which is plainly visible from Saint Peter's Square.*

Every year several thousand students who attend the centers of the Work throughout the world come to celebrate Easter in Rome. In 1980, during a meeting, one of them pointed out to John Paul II that Saint Peter's Square was crowned with statues of saints but that there was no image of our Lady.

"Maybe one could be set up, Holy Father", he suggested. To which the pope replied: "Very good, very good!"

When they told him about the incident, Don Álvaro asked the architect Javier Cotelo to think about where an image could be placed, a strategic point of the square that was capable of attracting attention. Javier drew up a plan that envisaged a mosaic at one corner of the Apostolic Palace. John Paul II liked the idea so much that he immediately ordered its execution.

In one of the rooms of your Roman headquarters we find the icon of the Black Madonna of Częstochowa with the pope's autograph.

It is a token of the paternal affection of John Paul II. For his seventieth birthday, Don Álvaro, on March 11, 1984, received at home this reproduction of Our Lady of Częstochowa with a few lines handwritten by the pontiff, brimming with affection for him. Everyone who met often with Pope Wojtyła noticed that he "knew how to love".

I will confide something else to you: three days after the death of John Paul II, Father Stanislaw presented me with one of his white cassocks, which we venerate today as a precious relic.

Your Excellency, you followed the activity of John Paul II very closely. Now that he is recognized as a saint, how can we sum up the value of his long pontificate?

The activity of John Paul II was so extensive and he was such an important figure that it is not possible to give any synthesis or summary.

His pontificate was something unique in a time frame spanning whole decades of our recent history. He showed, once again, with deeds, that the pope is the "servant of the servants of God", the tireless defender of the truth, the advocate of all men, in whose dignity he believed with all his might. He made Christ present in our time and brought mankind to seek in Jesus the answer to the ultimate questions about life.

John Paul II left us a wealth of teaching and a splendid example of pastoral charity. The aspect of his ministry that I would highlight is the impetus he gave toward a new evangelization through everyday life, through persons actively present in all fields of human endeavor, conducting themselves in a way consistent with the faith.

And what did you personally think when the miracle attributed to Blessed John Paul II was announced?

I thought once again of how Pope Wojtyła spent himself generously and unreservedly in the service of mankind. He brought us closer to God with his productive Magisterium: through his speeches, his writings, his images, and his many meaningful gestures. Everything about him pointed to Jesus Christ. Because his whole life was founded on an intimate communion with the Lord: it was enough to observe him as he was praying to understand the fruitfulness of his ministry.

John Paul II was a father close to all the faithful, to the Church and specifically, I can say, to this part of the Church that is the prelature of Opus Dei. I think that, with him, millions of people felt that they were "favorite sons" of the pope.

Gianfranco Svidercoschi

A PONTIFICATE THAT CHANGED THE CHURCH

Gianfranco Svidercoschi, born in Ascoli Piceno in 1936 of a family of distant Polish origin, began to work as a journalist at the age of sixteen (in the fifties you started right away): having served his apprenticeship as a sports writer, he moved on to the Italian press agency ANSA and worked the political beat.

In 1958 his editors had already decided to send him to Paris as a correspondent, but at around that time the health of Pius XII deteriorated to the point where there was no hope of his recovery. Then the director of ANSA changed the plan and asked young Svidercoschi to remain to help cover the "event". So it was that this promising journalist started to report on the Vatican.

There was no lack of work, because the death of Pope Pacelli was followed by the conclave, with the election of John XXIII, and then Vatican Council II.

During the council, Svidercoschi became acquainted with Karol Wojtyła. He turned to the young archbishop of Kraków to obtain some information. Subsequently he saw him often in Rome but got to know him better in 1977, when he had to conduct an investigation in Poland, six months after the incidents at the factory in Ursus, which in a way anticipated the birth of the *Solidarność* movement.

When Pope Paul VI died, and John Paul I soon after, Svidercoschi was one of the very few Vatican watchers who foresaw the possibility of the election of Cardinal Wojtyła. His reasoning was simple: the future pope would have to be a prelate from outside the Roman Curia; a moderate man, considering the postconciliar tensions that had come to a boil between "progressives" and "conservatives"; someone who spoke Italian well (but not necessarily an Italian), and a young man. ("The cardinals", he recalls, "were shocked by the death of John Paul I, who was sixty-five years old, and so they were looking for someone even younger.") In an interview on Swiss television, the journalist suggested, therefore, two names: "Wojtyła and Ratzinger"!

After the election of John Paul II, Svidercoschi continued to report on the Vatican until 1983, when he was appointed assistant manager of the newspaper *L'Osservatore romano*, a job he held for two years. In 1996, he collaborated with John Paul II on the book *Gift and Mystery*, in which the pope remembered his fiftieth anniversary as a priest (Wojtyła himself suggested the format of that book: he would play the role of the witness, leaving to Svidercoschi the job of narrator).

Moreover, with Cardinal Stanislaw Dziwisz, the former secretary of John Paul II, he has written two books, which have met with tremendous success: *A Life with Karol* (2008) and *"Ho vissuto con un santo"* (I lived with a saint) (2013). Both of these volumes are dedicated to Wojtyła and are a collection of memories of the current archbishop of Kraków. It is easy to understand that Svidercoschi came to know many facts and learned many new things about the man whom he considered his "favorite pope".

Mr. Svidercoschi, you followed closely—as a journalist and as a collaborator— the extraordinary pontificate of John Paul II. Could you give us a brief assessment of it?

When the pontificate of John Paul II began, the Church was immersed in postconciliar conflicts, which were echoed by divisions in the episcopate, in the clergy, and even among the lay people. The first fundamental thing that the pope did was to "relativize" those conflicts by orienting the Church toward the major objective of evangelization.

Evangelization looked to two levels: an "external" level that was directed toward peoples who did not yet know Christ, with particular regard to the East and more specifically to Asia, because the pope maintained that the future of the Church was at stake there. The second, "internal" level is the so-called "new evangelization": the faith has grown weak, especially in the West, and it is necessary to reevangelize the Church within it.

Another process that the pontiff set in motion was the process of the declericalization of the Church. Not all Vaticanists noticed this important project of his: in my opinion, since the time of the Council of Trent there has never been such a strong attempt to bring down—as the pope himself put it—the wall in front of the clergy, that clerical one-sidedness that was created with the Council of Trent in response to the Protestant Reformation. Pope Wojtyła did it by always assigning more importance to the aspects of communion that were more lay and more charismatic in comparison to the hierarchical and institutional aspects.

In this way, John Paul II brought to light new protagonists of the Church, to whom he turned as his favorite interlocutors: young people, women, and the new ecclesial movements. If this process is still underway, it is thanks to Wojtyła, who was their precursor. And if not everything has been accomplished yet, it is because the pope was not always followed by the hierarchy.

An example?

John Paul II profoundly appreciated the role of women in society and in the Church; he exalted the female genius to the highest degree, but his voice often remained isolated.

The pope's activity was not limited to the Catholic world.

That is true. Outside the Church there was a strong commitment of the pope in the field of ecumenism. Even though many difficulties had to be addressed on that front, which was certainly not his fault. Such problems arose with the decision by the Anglicans to open the priesthood to women. As for the Orthodox, once Communism was over, forms of nationalism broke out, and as a result the particular Churches, which were strictly controlled and suffocated by regimes that were unaccustomed to living in the modern world, found themselves sharing in that nationalistic exaltation, thus shutting themselves off from relations with the others. This is the case with the patriarchate of Moscow, which has accused the Church of "proselytism" because of her commitment to evangelization in its own territory.

Despite these problems, the pope accomplished a great deal; even with the Orthodox world. Take, for example, the visit to Greece: John Paul II went there at the invitation of the Greek government.

Initially the Orthodox Church scarcely tolerated his arrival. But from his first speech, the pope asked forgiveness for the past sins of Catholics against the Orthodox (in particular he referred to the Fourth Crusade that destroyed Constantinople), and the atmosphere was totally changed. And so today there is still a good relationship between the Catholic Church and the Orthodox Church of Greece.

The same can be said with respect to the Rumanian Orthodox Church, too. Everyone remembers the people shouting: "Unitade, unitade!" when the Holy Father met with the Orthodox patriarch of Rumania.

It is necessary to remember also the efforts of John Paul II in the dialogue with the other religions, particularly with the monotheistic religions. The pope was the one who did the most to bring about a rapprochement with the Jews. He was the first pontiff to enter a synagogue and to establish diplomatic relations with Israel. He condemned anti-Semitism with the harshest words. With his visit to Jerusalem and to the Wailing Wall, he made the Jewish world understand what the Catholic Church is and who her head is.

And with respect to the Muslims?

John Paul II, after the conflicts of the past, devoted himself tirelessly to relations with Islam, also. The first major event along the path of dialogue was his journey to Morocco, during which, in the stadium in Casablanca, he spoke to around eighty thousand young Muslims, impressing them by the way in which he presented himself and by the way in which he explained the reasons for the Christian faith, which are not necessarily in contrast with the reasons for the Muslim faith.

Wojtyła, in Damascus, was also the first pope in history to enter a mosque. Unfortunately, the advent of Islamic-inspired terrorism created new disturbances. Then came September 11, the first war in Afghanistan, the second war in Iraq. These events considerably complicated the dialogue with Islam.

But we have to remember one thing: John Paul II, with his peace-making attempt, kept the Muslim world from considering the war in Iraq a religious conflict between the Muslim world and the Christian world.

In speaking about wars, you touched on the "discourse about peace" that is a major concern of the "Church of Wojtyła": What can you add in this connection?

The Church of John Paul II recovered all her credibility and moral authority to preach justice and peace throughout the world.

At certain moments, the pope found himself alone in promoting the cause of peace. Even though apparently it ended in his defeat, because there was war, he was actually victorious: he touched hearts and succeeded in showing that the war was a mistake, and he managed not to exasperate further the conflicts between Christians and Muslims.

The massive attendance at his funeral, also in terms of diplomatic delegations from all the countries of the world, is the most obvious result of Wojtyła's whole life, which was dedicated to peace.

John Paul II left a Church that is more spiritual, a Church that is more of a family and a communion, where every baptized person is truly recognized for who he is and no one is marginalized. A Church that is more at peace with herself, because she has acknowledged the errors of the past; a Church that is more at peace with others, because her relations with the other religions are decidedly better than in the seventies of the past century; a Church that has been able to recover her credibility and, therefore, has truly become the standard-bearer of peace in the world.

But John Paul II was not a "pacifist" as the political left depicts him. Wojtyła was also the pope who approved of so-called "humanitarian intervention".

He himself, while visiting a parish, described himself as a man of peace but not a pacifist. In the case of the Persian Gulf, he totally ruled out war, but in the case of the Balkans he approved "humanitarian intervention". The pope asked for humanitarian intervention, even in the absence of a state of war, when it was a matter of saving a population and when it was possible to carry out a foreign, international intervention.

Nevertheless, as a matter of principle, he went much farther than the Second Vatican Council, which limited itself to arguing against war: John Paul II asserted that war can no longer be the means of regulating relations among States.

Can it be said that, thanks to John Paul II, the process of the secularization of the world has slowed and the Catholic Church has regained her right of citizenship in the political, cultural, and social sphere?

Cardinal Dziwisz, in the book *A Life with Karol*, stressed that John Paul II regained ground that the Church and Christians had lost over the centuries. The Church regained ground from the left; she won back intellectuals from the secularist culture, and also the youth, who were no longer afraid to profess their faith and to aim for holiness.

In this way, he vindicated the Church's right to be present in society, not to conquer it, but to offer it moral support. It is enough to read his speech to the European Parliament in order to see that he would be opposed to any sort of "occupation" of society by the Church. The pontiff did not think it possible to rebuild a "Christian society" in the immediate future, but he thought realistically about a new Church-State relationship in which the Church could have spaces of her own.

John Paul II demonstrated that secularization was not the "cemetery of religion" and that the modern world itself was not necessarily in conflict with the Church. Rather, the pope demonstrated that the Church can live face to face with the modern world and can help the modern world to develop in a positive direction. Let us not forget that the Church and the Gospel have been rooted in and have addressed "the modern world" at every moment of their history.

We have been talking thus far about a man of action, about the pope who left an indelible imprint on the history of the world and of the Church. Now I would like to know: When did you understand that Wojtyła was also, or first of all, a priest with a profound spirituality and a holy man?

One October evening in 1983, I was invited to supper by the pontiff, together with the chief editor of *L'Osservatore romano*, Mario Agnes.

While we were at table, Father Stanislaw told us the news that they had retrieved the body of Father Jerzy Popieluszko, the chaplain of Solidarity, who had been murdered eleven days earlier by officials of the Polish Communist security services.

The pope then asked whether he might retire to the chapel to pray, and I went with him. I prayed for Father Popieluszko with emotion, with my eyes closed, because I had been very well acquainted with him: a generous priest with great faith who was close to the people, a saint.

After a while, I reopened my eyes, and my gaze was transfixed by John Paul II: the intensity with which he prayed and the total involvement that he showed were impressive. He was truly in contact with the Most High!

What finally happened?

I stopped praying, because I was absolutely convinced that his prayer would be enough.

While visiting Wojtyła privately, I discovered his holiness: a sanctity of everyday life. Obviously there was also a heroic sanctity at the time of the assassination attempt, a mystical suffering at the time of the sufferings that preceded his death; but his was, first of all, an ordinary sanctity, lived out day by day in his behavior with others and in his humanity, which was so distinctive.

Is it true that John Paul II was also great company, a joyous man with a good sense of humor?

During our meetings, often at table, he surprised me by his ability to listen. And Wojtyła's other trait was, in fact, his sense of humor. He was witty and was able to smile.

In this connection, I would like to tell a little story that the pope himself related to me. In 1992, John Paul II was operated on for a tumor in his colon. While he was convalescing in Castel Gandolfo, he received, one day, a visit from a nuncio who was originally from Italy and at that time was working in Africa. The latter began to tell him at great length what was happening in the country where he was staying, but little by little as the conversation progressed, he interrupted himself several times to ask about the pope's health. And John Paul II repeatedly reassured him, answering that he was well. Finally the nuncio was convinced, so much so that, while saying goodbye to the pontiff, he remarked: "Your Holiness, you are truly well, better than before the operation!" At that John Paul II placed one hand on his shoulder and, looking him in the eyes, told him, "Your Excellency, why don't you have an operation, too?"

Today I feel so much nostalgia for his presence and for that sense of humor of his.

VII

Toward the Glory of the Altars

Angelo Amato

"A SAINT, AND SO TO BE IMITATED"

On December 19, 2002, the Salesian priest Angelo Amato was appointed secretary of the Congregation for the Doctrine of the Faith, while the prefect was still Cardinal Joseph Ratzinger, the future Pope Benedict XVI. Soon afterward, he was consecrated a bishop, on January 6, 2003, by the hands of John Paul II. Later on, he continued his service at the side of Cardinal William Joseph Levada from the United States.

On July 9, 2008, he was appointed prefect of the Congregation for the Causes of the Saints by Benedict XVI and was raised to the cardinalatial dignity on November 20, 2010. In this capacity, he in a way "returned the compliment" to the Polish pope: indeed, through his hands passed all the salient documents from the whole canonization process of Karol Wojtyła, which he ratified and presented to the latter's two successors on the Petrine throne: Pope Benedict and Pope Francis.

Your Eminence, on January 14, 2011, you called on the Holy Father for his signature on the decree of beatification of John Paul II, who in 1984 had appointed Cardinal Joseph Ratzinger prefect of the Congregation for the Doctrine of the Faith and, later on, appointed you secretary of the same congregation. How did you interpret this event connected with the pontiff of whom you were both close collaborators?

When I went to see Pope Benedict XVI for his signature on the decree, I found the Holy Father smiling. He was truly very happy about the end of the process and about the beatification. And also because the process had been so swift.

The fact that both Cardinal Ratzinger and I were among the closest collaborators of John Paul II obliged us all the more to respect very carefully the procedure for the beatification.

Someone might object that the process was conducted hastily and a bit superficially, but that was not the case. On the contrary, precisely out of respect for the pope, we did things correctly and scrupulously, in order to avoid future complaints of negligence.

During the whole process, you, Your Eminence, observed the strictest confidentiality. But today could you reveal to us your personal feelings: Knowing John Paul II well, were you convinced of his sanctity?

I was thoroughly convinced of the sanctity of John Paul II even before the process began. His virtuous life was recognized throughout the world: he had a great faith and boundless trust in Divine Providence. After living and suffering under two totalitarian regimes, Nazism and Communism, with his great faith he saw the false ideologies crumble and good triumph over evil.

In the second place, his sanctity is connected also with his missionary spirit: I see this pope as a great evangelizer of the world. In every journey he made, he proclaimed Jesus Christ and the merciful grace of the Lord.

This reputation for sanctity grew after his death: just look at Saint Peter's Square, at the endless lines of people from all over who come to pray at his tomb. Moreover, testimonies frequently arrive from various parts of the world describing graces and temporal and spiritual favors received through his intercession.

Do you pray sometimes, too, at the tomb of Pope Wojtyła in Saint Peter's?

Of course. Frequently. I went there first when it was located in the Vatican Grottos, and now I go to the new location within the basilica. Sometimes alone, sometimes I accompany other people.

It is always an inspiration to pray at the tomb of John Paul II, because of the help he can give us in our work.

As early as December 2009, Benedict XVI approved the publication of the decree on the heroicity of the virtues of John Paul II. Can you explain for us the chief virtues characterizing the new saint?

The canonical virtues on which a Servant of God is evaluated are the theological virtues of faith, hope, and charity, and the cardinal virtues. But I would emphasize the pope's great faith. From this faith sprang the other virtues.

In what way was the process of John Paul II different from others?

His case was facilitated in two ways. First of all, the abrogation of the usual five-year waiting period for the process to begin. Secondly: the congregation gave preferential treatment to this process, thus avoiding interference with other causes on the waiting list.

Yet, it is worth repeating, the cause was conducted with the same rigor as all the others. No allowances were made with regard to procedural correctness.

Did the media pressure—which reflected both the expectations of so many people who wanted Wojtyła to be santo subito, *a saint immediately, and also the adverse opinions—influence the process?*

These pressures helped make those responsible for conducting the process particularly careful and prudent. You might say that their influence favored an extremely scrupulous analysis and verification of the documents.

The Church is very sensitive to the symbolism of dates. Was canonizing John Paul II on Divine Mercy Sunday the right choice?

I think so. The date chosen was the Sunday on which the Mercy of Our Lord Jesus Christ is celebrated. And I am certain that John Paul II, the pope who solemnized this feast at the inspiration of Saint Faustina Kowalska, was delighted with this choice: as already happened with his beatification, he will find that Sunday to be the most propitious context in which to celebrate his glorification in heaven.

Again in connection with the beatification, a happy coincidence has been noted: in 2011 the Sunday after Easter coincided with May 1.

The pope, who once worked as a laborer and knew physical weariness and dedicated three fundamental magisterial documents to the topic of work, was beatified on the day of the feast of workers. It was an extraordinary sign, a providential coincidence. These are the so-called "elegant touches of Divine Providence".

From the special observation post of the congregation that you direct, Your Eminence, can you tell us how the faithful experienced, or ought to have experienced, the time during which the Church brought to light the sanctity of Pope Wojtyła?

The time in which a canonization process develops is an opportunity for those employed in the work and for the faithful to become better acquainted with the figure of the future saint and also to further their personal sanctification: let us not forget that the saints are persons not just to contemplate but also and most importantly to imitate.

Marie Simon Pierre Normand

"JOHN PAUL II HAD THE LAST WORD"

There are no saints or Blesseds without miracles. It is true that paradise is full of unknown saints, but when the Church investigates "officially", before declaring someone Blessed or a saint, she "demands" a sign from heaven. This sign must be a miracle that has taken place through the intercession of a Servant of God (in the case of a beatification process) or of a Blessed (for his canonization).

Monsignor Slawomir Oder, postulator in the process of John Paul II, as he himself relates in this volume, received a great many testimonies of presumed miracles that occurred after the death of the pontiff. But for the cause of beatification and, then, of canonization, he chose the two cases that seemed to him most significant.

Let us meet Sister Marie Simon Pierre Normand, the French nun who was miraculously cured through the intercession of Pope Wojtyła. She was suffering from the same illness, Parkinson's disease.

The Medical Board of the Congregation for the Causes of the Saints established that her case is inexplicable from the human, scientific perspective. Moreover, the Theological Commission certified the causal connection between the invocation of the intercession of the Blessed (the prayers of her sisters in religion to the Polish pope) and the healing as a manifestation of Divine Grace.

This inexplicable healing allowed John Paul II to be proclaimed Blessed on May 1, 2011.

Sister Marie Simon Pierre, how did your vocation to consecrated life come about in a laicized, de-Christianized France?

My vocation originated in the domestic hearth of a family from Northern France; they were all practicing Catholics, especially on my mother's side.

I was born in 1961 in Rumilly-en-Cambrésis, the oldest of five children: I have three sisters and a brother. From the time when I was little, I used to go to Mass every Sunday with my mom. My childhood and adolescence were permeated with a great spirit of family unity, generosity, and mutual support. At the age of twelve, I received Confirmation: on that day I experienced the grace of the Lord, and, in the secret of my heart, I promised to give myself to him forever.

Later on, in 1977, I made my first pilgrimage to Lourdes. There I discerned a very strong call to religious life. Surely guided by the Lord, I went to the baths and had the grace of bathing there: I emerged from the water completely transformed. Mary always leads us to her Son, and deep down I understood that I had to follow her.

Why did you choose the Little Sisters of the Catholic Maternities?

For me the choice was very clear. I said Yes to Jesus to serve the family with all my being, to serve and defend life. Therefore, in 1980, I enrolled in courses in infant care, and, in September 1981, I received a diploma as an assistant.

And since I was attracted by everything having to do with family life, I sensed the desire to work with the Little Sisters of the Catholic Maternities so as to get to know them better and to discern whether that was the place to which the Lord was calling me. In mid-October of that same year, I was accepted as an infant care assistant. And in 1982, on Holy Thursday night, I responded to the Lord's call, giving my life for the cause of Life.

On September 14, 1982, I entered the postulancy with the Little Sisters, and on July 6, 1983, as I made my oblation, I took the name Marie Simon Pierre and began my novitiate. From 1988 to 1992, I studied in Lyon to earn a nursing diploma. Finally, in 1993, I made final profession.

Let us speak now about John Paul II. How did you react to the election of a Polish pope?

When he was elected, I was only seventeen years old, and the fact that he was Polish did not cause any reaction in me.

Well, then, for Sister Marie Simon Pierre, a consecrated religious, what did the pontificate of John Paul II mean?

He was truly close to everyone; he was willing to go all through the world to meet people, as Pope Francis ceaselessly recalls.

The duration of his pontificate is impressive. By the way, they talk about John Paul II as a "giant", a "giant of prayer", and an example of faith for all of us. He belonged completely to God and to Mary.

Inspired with the fervor of the saints, he launched the World Youth Days and established the World Day of Consecrated Life (February 2). He also prepared the post-synodal apostolic exhortation on consecrated life (March 25, 1996), which offers us religious so much light for an in-depth study of our state of life.

The last years of the pontiff were a great trial, because of his illnesses, first and foremost Parkinson's disease. You too, in 2001, were diagnosed with Parkinson's. What was it like sharing in the same sufferings as the pope?

When they diagnosed my illness, it made me uneasy to look at John Paul II on television: his image reminded me of my sickness.

Nevertheless, I always remained very close to him in prayer. I admired his humility, strength, and courage. His example and witness of total abandonment in giving himself to others, continuing his ministry no matter what, strengthened me in my faith and in my struggle to accept and to offer up my suffering.

I realized that the pope could understand what I was going through. Today I can say that it was a daily struggle, but my one desire was to live it in loving acceptance of the Father's will.

At Easter in 2005, I would have liked to receive the blessing of our Holy Father during the live TV broadcast. His health was worsening day by day, and I sensed that this would be the last time I would see him. For the whole morning, I prepared for that encounter, aware that it would be very difficult for me: he had given me a precise idea of my own future in the years to come, with one difference: in comparison with John Paul II, I was still relatively young. But an unexpected, surely providential fact did not allow me to see him: I was detained in service.

Because you continued to work, despite your illness?

Yes, I still did, obviously at a pace I could manage to keep up. I no longer worked actively as a nurse: they had assigned to me the position of supervisor in the maternity ward. I did a lot of things with the computer, but, whenever I could, I looked after families with disabled children or helped nursing mothers: those were the moments in which I could offer some advice and listen when they confided in me.

What did you experience on April 2, 2005, the day of the pope's death?

That evening our whole community gathered to follow together on television the prayer vigil on Saint Peter's Square, which was broadcast by KTO, the television channel of the diocese of Paris. And so my sisters and I heard immediately the news about the death of John Paul II.

At that moment, everything changed for me: it was a blow to me; I had lost a friend, a dear person who understood me and gave me the strength and energy to go forward.

In the days that followed—until April 8, the day of his funeral— things improved a bit: I felt a great emptiness, because of his physical absence, but at the same time inside me I was sure that he was still present.

On May 13, 2005, Pope Benedict XVI announced a special dispensation so as to initiate the cause for the beatification of John Paul II. Were you informed that on the following day all the sisters of your congregation started to implore Karol Wojtyła to intercede for your cure?

Yes, I knew immediately that all the Little Sisters were praying for me to John Paul II. Mother Marie-Marc also telephoned me to ask me whether I agreed with this initiative of hers. After a moment of silence and emotion, I accepted, solely with the intention of being able to keep serving life and to continue my mission to families.

Feeling supported by the prayers of all my sisters in religion was important to me. And on the evening of May 14, the entire community actually started a perpetual novena to ask for the miracle of my cure, as a small contribution toward the cause of the pope's beatification. From that day on, even when I was physically in pain and exhausted, a verse from Scripture constantly echoed inside me: verse 40 of chapter 10 of the Gospel of Saint John, which reads: "If you believe, you will see the glory of God."

Could you elaborate on the details of your cure?

The clinical signs of the disease worsened rapidly in the weeks after the pope's death. On June 1, I was unable to tolerate the pain, because it had greatly increased; the tremors had intensified, so that it became very difficult for me to stand, and I could scarcely move any more. I was losing all my strength.

On the afternoon of June 2—exactly two months after the death of John Paul II—I asked my superior, who at that time was Sister Marie Thomas, to assign another sister to the maternity ward, since I was now exhausted.

In my heart I asked the pope to help me accept the use of a wheelchair, on a day that seemed to me to be drawing near; I promised him that my religious consecration would not weaken. Nothing, not even the disease, could prevent me from living life to the full. I would continue to offer my life for the cause of Life.

The superior listened to me attentively but asked me to wait until I had returned from the pilgrimage to Lourdes, which I was supposed to make in the month of August; she reminded me that all of our communities were praying for my cure through the intercession of the Holy Father.

Then she added: "John Paul II has not yet said the last word."

She then asked me to write the pope's name on a piece of paper, but I could not do it. But she insisted: on the third try I wrote "John Paul II", but my writing was so illegible that we were both deeply grieved and remained together for a long time in silence, praying.

When did you notice that you were cured?

That same evening, between 21:30 and 21:45 hours, I felt like writing, and I noticed that my writing had become normal again.

Then I went to bed. I awoke at 4:30: I jumped out of bed, without feeling any pain, and went downstairs to the oratory of the community house to pray before the Blessed Sacrament. I was enveloped with a great peace, a sensation of well-being. Then, still before the Blessed Sacrament, I began to meditate on the Mysteries of Light, which were added to the Rosary by John Paul II: I remained in prayer until 6:00.

At that time, I thought of joining my sisters in religion in the chapel for prayer, which is followed by Morning Prayer and the Eucharist. I went about fifty-five yards and realized that, while I was walking, my left arm, which until then had been entirely immobilized because of the disease, had started to swing. Moreover, my body felt very nimble, a flexibility I had not experienced in a long time.

During Mass, peace and joy once again permeated my heart. And at the end of the liturgy, I was convinced I had been cured: I am left-handed, and my left hand was not trembling at all; my face had been transformed.

It was the morning of June 3, the day of the Solemnity of the Sacred Heart: a feast that was so dear to John Paul II. I began to write again, and at noon I stopped taking all my medications.

In the afternoon I told my superior, Sister Marie Thomas, about everything: together we agreed to keep secret what had happened until June 7, that is, until an already scheduled visit to the doctor.

What was your doctor's reaction?

As I said, long before then I had made an appointment to see the neurologist on that day. When he saw me, the doctor observed with amazement the complete disappearance of all the symptoms of the disease. It was difficult to convince him that I was in good condition, considering also the fact that for five days I had no longer been taking any medications.

After the visit, all our communities were informed of my cure, and on that June 7 they began to thank God for having answered our prayers. I also informed my parents, my other relatives, and my closest friends. But for two years afterward, we all kept what had happened strictly confidential so as not to interfere with the beatification process.

How did your life change, on the spiritual level, too, after June 3, 2005?

I had had not only a physical healing: the grace that I received affected my whole being, even the depths of my soul. I often repeated: "I was sick and I am healed."

I remain one Little Sister among others, and it is important for me to perform my service for the mothers and the babies with joy and simplicity.

What the Lord granted me to experience that night through the intercession of John Paul II is a great mystery that is difficult to explain in words, because it is so great and so strong. I had the experience of a second birth, of a new life.

Nothing is as it was before. My interior life has been turned upside down and, thus, has become deeper. Today I am much more drawn to the Eucharist and to Eucharistic adoration, and I never miss praying the Rosary, either. On the second day of every month, at 9:00 P.M., I withdraw in prayer and remain that way for a long time, both to give thanks for what the Lord has done in me and also to intercede for others (requests for prayer arrive now from all over the world).

The Lord continues to give me love and special concern for the least ones, the weakest, for instance, disabled children, whom our world often rejects but whom John Paul II loved so much.

And let us not forget that this healing is an event that concerns not just me but the Church and the world. For our religious family, it is a special encouragement to persevere in our mission in the Church, which is to proclaim, serve, and celebrate the Gospel of Life through our presence in France and Senegal, that is, in the two countries where we have our works; it is an encouragement to live out the apostolate of mercy among young people and families.

Furthermore, I carry in my heart, in a particular way, broken families and Parkinson's patients.

What did it mean for you to have an "active part" in the beatification process of a pope?

Ever since I agreed that my congregation should pray for my cure through the intercession of John Paul II, I have always said that, if our prayers were answered, I would cooperate thoroughly with whatever procedures were required. And I have done so, full of gratitude and desiring intensely that Pope Wojtyła should soon be declared Blessed, and then a saint, so that the world might believe, so that human life might be respected and all those who work in the service of life might be encouraged.

There is no doubt about it: my country, France, needed to receive this new "visit" from John Paul II so as not to lose its own roots.

What effect has being "chosen by God" had on you?

God works signs, God blesses, God shows his power over life through cures. Our Heavenly Father knows that men still need signs in order to believe. The beatification and the canonization of John Paul II are a blessing for the Church and for the world; a marvelous sign that the Lord has granted to us in order to encourage us to proclaim the Way, the Truth, and the Life that he is himself, in our society, which would appear to be ensnared by the culture of death.

And, as I have already said, this sign was perceived very strongly in my religious institute as an incentive to promote forcefully respect for every human being from the moment of conception until natural death.

What were your feelings when you heard the news about the approval of the miracle obtained through the intercession of Blessed John Paul II that opened the way for his canonization?

Tremendous joy and profound gratitude to the Lord. My heart sings the *Magnificat*, it is truly filled with joy and thanksgiving.

Floribeth Mora Díaz

"A VOICE TOLD ME
TO GET UP FROM BED"

After the beatification of John Paul II on May 1, 2011, in order to proclaim him a saint, it was "sufficient"—as Cardinal Amato and Monsignor Oder have explained in this book—to certify a new miracle that occurred after that date. This miracle did take place, precisely on that date, in Costa Rica, in Latin America, which the Polish pope loved so much.

On that continent, where more than 40 percent of all the Catholics in the world live, he had made his first international apostolic journey, only four months after his election. In 1983, he also visited Costa Rica, a small country that has a little more than four and a half million inhabitants, a politically and socially stable country that is Catholic by nature and profoundly Marian. It was no accident that news of the miracle was welcomed with great joy by President Laura Chinchilla Miranda and was posted very prominently on the website of the government.

The recipient of the miracle, Floribeth Mora Díaz, the wife of Edwin Antonio Arce Abarca and the mother of four children (a fifth died), lives in a little town called Dulce Nombre de Jesús.

At the time of the miracle, in 2011, she was forty-seven years old. She was a healthy woman, but on April 8 of that year she suddenly experienced a very severe headache. She was brought to the emergency room of Max Peralta Hospital in Cartago and was promptly admitted to the intensive care unit of Calderón Guardia Hospital in the capital, San José.

There the doctors informed her of the diagnosis as though it were a death sentence: "A burst aneurysm of the right cerebral artery with hemorrhage." Moreover, the surgeon at the hospital was not able to insert a stent, because the artery affected by the aneurysm was located in an inaccessible part of the brain. In that situation, the husband was advised to take his wife back home. Edwin Antonio was desperate and, as he related afterward, turned to John Paul II: "Holy Father, I pray you to help me and intercede with God for the healing of my wife." In addition to this prayer, the husband made a concrete gesture: "We had set up in the hallway a little altar in honor of the Holy Child, with the inscription 'Jesus, I trust in you.' Upon returning from the hospital, I placed beside it also an image of Pope Wojtyła."

At home, Floribeth's situation was truly dramatic: any new hemorrhage would in all probability have caused bodily paralysis or death.

At that time, preparations were being made in Rome for the beatification of John Paul II. Despite her severe sharp pains in the head, the woman wanted to watch the beatification Mass on television, praying to the pope that she might be cured. The next morning, she awoke without any pain. To her great amazement, she could walk and speak, and she told her husband: "Something happened!"

A miracle had occurred. The doctors observed a scientifically inexplicable fact: there was no longer any trace of the aneurysm in the patient's brain.

After her extraordinary healing, Señora Mora Díaz went to a church in Cartago where a relic of John Paul was exposed, which had been donated by Cardinal Dziwisz, and she told the whole story to the priest, Father Donald.

She also sent an e-mail to the postulation of the cause of canonization of John Paul II. There her account, which was read for the first time on February 23, 2012, was immediately considered "interesting" and worth further investigation by the postulator. Monsignor Oder therefore took steps to request from Señora Mora Díaz all the clinical documentation concerning her case. And to complete the assessments, he invited her to Rome to submit to all the examinations necessary for a scientific evaluation.

After the evidence was gathered by the postulation, her case was submitted to examination by the Congregation for the Causes of the Saints: in this phase, the medical board declared her cure inexplicable from a scientific viewpoint; and finally, the evaluations of the theologians and cardinal members of the dicastery were positive.

Thus the miracle of Floribeth Mora Díaz opened the way to proclaim John Paul II a saint. But here is the account of the woman who received the miracle.

Señora Floribeth, how do you want to be presented to the readers?

You can present me as a normal woman, because I continue to be what I was. The one thing that changed in my life is the schedule of meetings in which I agree to participate so as to give testimony to the greatness and the mercy of our Heavenly Father.

Interiorly, the most remarkable change concerns my relationship with God, the conscious resolution that I made after my cure to serve him in everything that he arranges for me. In short, I continue to be the same Floribeth, but more full of God.

Most of your life coincided with the pontificate of John Paul II. What was your connection with that pope?

I admired John Paul II, the person that he was, from the time I was young. I was attracted by his great simplicity, the humility he allowed to shine through, the special charism he manifested in dealing with everybody.

It would be meaningful to hear directly from you the account of your illness, how you reacted when you learned of the terrible diagnosis.

I was forty-seven years old when I became ill.

It all happened like lightning under clear skies: from one day to the next I found myself in a situation where I was in danger of death. My head started to burst unexpectedly. At the moment when it happened, I could not understand, because I had always been in good health; I had gone to hospitals only to give birth to my five children. And so, when my diagnosis was brain damage, I could not believe it, not even afterward, when they told me that I had not much time to live.

Fear, however, made its way into my mind as I saw the sadness on the faces of my children and my husband; and it increased little by little as my physical deterioration became evident.

Did your faith ever decrease?

Never. In every situation I always relied on God. And I prayed for
the intercession of John Paul II.

*On May 1, 2011, at two o'clock in the early morning, local time, the live
television broadcast of the beatification Mass of Pope Wojtyła began in Costa
Rica. Did you watch it?*

Certainly, for me it was a much awaited event. And I didn't miss
a moment of it, lying in bed and watching the TV, over which I
had taped a photo of the pope on the day of his election, when on
the balcony of Saint Peter's he stretched out his arms to embrace the
world. And if I had not been so ill, if I had had at least a little strength,
I would have gone also to the vigil in the National Stadium, where so
many people had gathered, among them my family.

But it was not easy: I was overwhelmed by atrocious spasms and
totally immobilized. And so while taping that photo I asked John
Paul II to help: "If you will, help me to be cured, intercede for me
with the Lord: tell him that I do not want to die." I also asked for the
grace to be able to remain awake for the duration of the Mass. And
so it was. Then I was enfolded in a profound sleep.

Why did you decide to commend yourself specifically to him?

Because I always believed, even when he was alive, that he was a
saint, since I always saw him full of God. I have no doubt that John
Paul II is close to God and that he intercedes for us with our Lord.

When and how did you notice that your prayers had been answered?

When I awoke the next morning at around 9:00. I found myself
alone in my room. I glanced at the portrait of the pope to greet him
and made the sign of the cross. At that precise moment I heard an
interior voice that told me to get up from bed.

I felt in the depths of my soul that I had to obey, and I had the
strength to do so. I then felt a great peace, and the incredible thing

was that I was no longer afraid. I think the physical healing happened in a second phase: the Lord first worked on my spirit, giving me great peace and assurance of my cure.

Did you recognize that voice; could you say whose it was?

It was like his voice, the voice of John Paul II, which was very quietly encouraging me: "Get up! Be not afraid!" And while looking at the photo, I also had the sense that his hands, which were extended toward me, moved upward as he made his request.

How did your family and friends react?

My husband, when he saw me come into the kitchen and then start puttering around, became thoroughly exasperated and sent me back to bed!

At that moment I did not tell him what had happened, because I understood that he would have thought I was crazy. I just told him that I felt stronger and that my heart was full of new peace and confidence. But I was not the one to say that I felt well; it was obvious that at the physical level, too, a change had taken place, as was demonstrated by the following clinical examination, to everyone's great surprise.

When you say "everyone's", you of course include the physicians who were treating you and who had predicted that you were nearing the end of your life?

The doctors thought at first that they had attributed to me by mistake the diagnostic results of another patient, but as soon as they determined that that was not the case, they were plainly overcome with utter amazement, because they, more than anyone else, realized that they were witnessing something miraculous.

My friends and acquaintances—all the people who knew me and had seen me sick—were now astonished by the fact that I was restored to health so rapidly.

Everyone was somewhat overwhelmed with amazement and great joy in those days.

Did you say that you were subjected afterward to further tests?

Yes, systematically, and also at the request of the postulation. Two successive MRIs performed in November 2011 and in May 2012 proved the total and "spontaneous" disappearance of the aneurysm.

The Lord granted you a great favor; did you wonder what significance it might have?

Certainly: this great miracle has a lot to tell us, and not just me personally.

We are going through truly difficult times, in which there is a lack of faith. If you ask me, this miracle occurred so that when we learn about it, we might improve the quality of our lives and lift our sights to heaven and be able to tell that God exists, that he is Life, and that without God there is no true life.

Without faith, without hope, none of these marvels would have happened. But it is necessary always to have faith in the One whom we do not see now, although in our hearts and minds we know that he exists.

How do you see the new saint?

As I have already said, I admired John Paul II profoundly even when he was alive among us. I continue to believe even more that he intercedes for us now that he is no longer with us but is experiencing eternal happiness with God.

The date of the pope's canonization will go down in history as April 27, 2014, but for me he always was a saint.

Thank you!

I thank you and your readers for thinking of me. Let us pray that everything that has happened may be for the honor and glory of God.

Slawomir Oder

"I FEEL IT IS MY DUTY TO TESTIFY
TO THE GIFTS I RECEIVED AS POSTULATOR"

Slawomir Oder was born in Chelmza, Poland, in 1960 and was ordained a priest twenty-nine years later in Pelplin. From then on his life took him far away from his homeland, to Rome: there he studied at the Pontifical Lateran University, where he earned a doctorate in *utroque iure* [in both canon law and civil law]; there he was an instructor at the major seminary; there, finally, for many years he has worked in the Tribunal of Appeals of the Vicariate of Rome. In April 2013, Pope Francis appointed him judicial vicar of the Ordinary Tribunal of the diocese of Rome.

Even while working abroad, he never forgot Poland; he collaborated with the Congregation for the Causes of the Saints as postulator in the beatification processes of the Polish priests Stefan Frelichowski and Wladyslaw Kornilowicz and of Mother Elzbieta Czacka.

The life of this young priest changed radically when Cardinal Camillo Ruini, the pope's vicar for the diocese of Rome, assigned him the job of postulator in the beatification and canonization process of John Paul II. For Monsignor Oder, that was the beginning of "the adventure of my life", which, as he confides, enriched him as a priest and as a man. On the occasion of the upcoming canonization, Monsignor Oder recalls the intense years of the process and explains for us also the devotion to the new saint.

For you, as postulator of the cause of beatification of John Paul II, 2011 was a special year. How did you experience it?

Yes, indeed, 2011 was a very special year: on May 1, the beatification ceremony of John Paul II was performed, and, on October 22, the first liturgical feast of the new Blessed was celebrated. After six years of intense work, I had arrived at an important milestone: finally the Church was able to offer this splendid example of his to the people of God and to the world.

But that year completed only the first stage, because the process did not stop. From the theological perspective, the terms "blessed" and "saint" do not change the fact of sanctity. What changes, however, is the extent of the cult: in the case of a Blessed, the cult proposed is local; in the case of a saint, the cult is universal. The involvement of papal authority changes, too: the declaration of sainthood, that is, canonization, involves the infallibility of the pontiff.

This does not mean, though, that in order to canonize a Blessed it is necessary to repeat the process, does it?

The process to certify the heroicity of virtues is not repeated, because that heroicity has already been determined. But in order to reach the finish line of canonization, the praxis of the Church requires a second miracle, which must take place after the day of the beatification.

Let us go back to the beginning, that is, to the process of beatification. What highlights made an impression on you?

Surely the moment when the cardinal vicar for the diocese of Rome entrusted this task to me. It was on May 13, 2005, the same day as the visit of Pope Benedict XVI to the Basilica of Saint John Lateran, his first meeting with the clergy of Rome; the same day on which the Holy Father announced his decision to dispense John Paul II from the traditional waiting period of five years before initiating a process.

It was a great sign of the cardinal's confidence in me. I am judicial vicar, and then I was already working as president of the Tribunal of Appeals of the Vicariate of Rome. Therefore, this new reality was added to my daily work routine. This meant a major professional challenge, but also a personal one, because I had to reorganize my life completely.

Another unforgettable moment was the opening of the process, on June 28 (still in the year 2005), the day of the Solemnity of Saints Peter and Paul, in the presence of representatives of the local Churches, among them the Church of Rome and the Polish Church, but also of the sister Churches such as the Patriarchate of Constantinople. This

way of opening the process corresponded to the ecumenical dimension, which was one of the most important features of the pontificate
of John Paul II.

Other highlights?

What followed then was the normal procedural work, collecting
documents and meeting with the witnesses. But among the witnesses
there were persons who, together with the pope, helped change
contemporary history; and simply from the human perspective, con-
tacting these great protagonists was a beautiful and very enriching
experience.

I remember, furthermore, shortly after the process began, when
we received news from France about the healing of Sister Marie
Simon Pierre, which was then recognized by the Church as miraculous. Hearing that news was a very emotional experience for me,
also, because the nun had been suffering from Parkinson's disease, the
same disease that afflicted John Paul II during his last years on earth.

Not to mention the emotions of the various stages in the process:
the submission of the *Positio*, the recognition of the miracle, and the
promulgation of the decree on the heroicity of virtues. But the most
gratifying moment for me was the exchange of the sign of peace
with Pope Benedict XVI during the Mass of beatification: I became
a sharer in the great joy of the Holy Father, who from the beginning unfailingly accompanied this process with his goodwill, with his
prayer, and with a series of homilies, citations, and discreet but very
careful interventions, with which he made his indirect contribution
to the cause.

And immediately after the celebration, while I was leaving Saint
Peter's Square, I was able to touch with my hands and breathe in
deeply the enthusiasm of the people who had gathered, truly from all
over the world. I saw the Church being festive, and then I felt profound gratitude to God and great personal satisfaction.

What did you get out of "investigating" the sanctity of John Paul II?

The process became the adventure of looking closely at the story of a
priest, because despite the fact that John Paul II was pope and before
that a cardinal and a bishop, he always remained first of all a priest,

that is to say, he lived out his whole life in an authentically priestly spirit. And so "investigating" Karol Wojtyła meant confronting a splendid example of the priesthood, which made me enthusiastic, strengthened my vocation, and in many ways stimulated my personal growth.

According to the established practice, after the beatification, the cult was supposed to be limited to Italy and Poland. But we heard reports of requests coming from other parts of the world to authorize the cult of John Paul II. Can you confirm them?

It is true that beatification pertains to the local Church, but from the start, the Congregation for Divine Worship and the Discipline of the Sacraments gave local episcopates the option of asking that same congregation for permission to celebrate the feast of the new Blessed, considering the worldwide dimension of the cult of a personage like John Paul II.

Many episcopates took advantage of this possibility and inscribed his feast day in the local liturgical calendar.

Every day thousands of believers pray at the tomb of the saintly pope at Saint Peter's. But there is also the phenomenon of the pilgrimages of his relics.

All this happened spontaneously, initially with the requests of individual persons who asked for a holy picture with a relic *ex indumentis* (from the clothing) of the Blessed.

After the cult was allowed and it became possible to dedicate churches to Blessed John Paul, many bishops, too, asked for relics so as to be able to have them in their dioceses, so as to present them for public veneration in a church or a seminary.

Later on, to continue conceptually the style of the pontificate—the itinerant style of the pilgrim of love and peace—the relics of the pope started to go on pilgrimage. The first "outing" was organized by the 2011 World Youth Day in Madrid, with a vial of the blood of John Paul II. Here the relic was the symbol of this event before being brought to Mexico.

What is the value of the cult of relics? Isn't there a danger that someone might misinterpret it?

The danger exists, but we always need to remember that this is not about some magical aspect: the relics are a sign of the presence of the saint in our midst, a concrete, historical sign. It is not a magical reality, but a reminder of the person's values and of his teaching.

I must say that all these experiences of the pilgrimages have left me greatly edified, because the people were prepared correctly, with catechesis, with a presentation of the pope's teaching.

What was the role of the postulation after the beatification?

As I have already said, the canonization did not require a reopening of the process on the heroicity of virtues, because that whole very demanding aspect was now history.

In the period following the beatification, my work consisted in "vigilance", watching so as to be able to identify a miraculous case that could initiate the process for canonization.

Meanwhile, the figure of the postulator became a point of reference for the whole spiritual movement connected with the desire to become better acquainted with the message of the life and the holiness of Pope Wojtyła.

John Paul II used to say that every gift is a responsibility. Therefore, after the beatification, I quite willingly took part in a great many initiatives so as to make my contribution and to promote an ever better knowledge of the pope and of his teachings. I felt the specific duty to share with others all that I had received in the years I had spent as postulator, in which I had a continual experience of grace.

Could you tell us something about the miracles attributed to John Paul II that were brought to attention of the postulation?

I can say that there were a great number of reports, which started before the beatification and never stopped even after it.

Letters and testimonials about graces received continued to arrive at my office.

In a necessary work of skimming, I concentrated my attention on several particularly interesting and significant letters. Finally, I focused on one case, about which I asked the witness to produce all the documentation possible. The first examination was positive, and so we could proceed immediately with the investigation of the miracle.

Generally speaking, how are miracles certified?

The first examination is carried out by me in the postulation, obviously in collaboration with the experts. Once the importance of a case is ascertained, a canonical process is instituted, during which all available documentation is collected, then the so-called *positio* is prepared, which is to be submitted to the Congregation for the Causes of the Saints. Within the congregation, the Medical Board establishes whether or not a case is explicable from the perspective of human sciences. In contrast, the Theological Commission has to certify the causal connection between the invocation of the Blessed's intercession and the effect obtained through a manifestation of Divine Grace.

Can you comment for us, from your perspective, on the miracle that made possible the canonization of John Paul II?

You mean the healing of the cerebral aneurysm of Floribeth Mora Díaz, a woman from Costa Rica.

Her illness was diagnosed in the period before the beatification. The doctors saw no possibility of a recovery for her. The aneurysm was located in an inoperable area of the brain.

During the rite of beatification, which the woman watched on television, she and her family invoked the intercession of the new Blessed. The answer came immediately: the woman heard an interior voice that urged her to get up from bed. She obeyed and immediately returned to her domestic duties and her normal activities. All the signs of her illness disappeared without a trace.

After the testimony reached me in Rome, I looked into the case, and then I asked the bishop of San José, in Costa Rica, to institute the tribunal to instruct the process on the alleged miracle.

In late 2012, the documentation was forwarded to the Congregation for the Causes of the Saints and was the object of a very detailed inquiry that went through various stages of verification.

When were the results of the process forwarded to Pope Francis?

The Holy Father, at the request of the prefect of the Congregation for the Causes of the Saints, authorized the publication of the decree recognizing the miracle during the audience granted to Cardinal Angelo Amato on July 5, 2013. Thus the path to canonization was opened.

At the start of our conversation, you recalled the beatification ceremony of John Paul II. What were your feelings as you prepared for the canonization?

The preparations for the canonization turned out to be very demanding, also, but nothing will ever remove from my heart my gratitude to God for having granted me the grace to live through this adventure and for having helped me to bring to completion the mandate entrusted to me by my superiors. Together with this gratitude, I will carry with me an immense joy, thinking of the good that John Paul II will continue to accomplish forever, as a saint, by interceding with God on behalf of his people!

VIII

Finally Blessed!

His Holiness Pope Benedict XVI

HOMILY ON THE OCCASION OF THE
BEATIFICATION OF JOHN PAUL II

Sunday, May 1, 2011

Dear Brothers and Sisters,

Six years ago we gathered in this Square to celebrate the funeral of
Pope John Paul II. Our grief at his loss was deep, but even greater was
our sense of an immense grace which embraced Rome and the whole
world: a grace which was in some way the fruit of my beloved predecessor's entire life, and especially of his witness in suffering. Even
then we perceived the fragrance of his sanctity, and in any number of
ways God's People showed their veneration for him. For this reason,
with all due respect for the Church's canonical norms, I wanted his
cause of beatification to move forward with reasonable haste. And
now the longed-for day has come; it came quickly because this is
what was pleasing to the Lord: John Paul II is blessed!

I would like to offer a cordial greeting to all of you who on this
happy occasion have come in such great numbers to Rome from
all over the world—cardinals, patriarchs of the Eastern Catholic
Churches, brother bishops and priests, official delegations, ambas-
sadors and civil authorities, consecrated men and women and lay
faithful, and I extend that greeting to all those who join us by radio
and television.

Today is the Second Sunday of Easter, which Blessed John Paul II
entitled Divine Mercy Sunday. The date was chosen for today's celebration because, in God's providence, my predecessor died on the
vigil of this feast. Today is also the first day of May, Mary's month,
and the liturgical memorial of Saint Joseph the Worker. All these
elements serve to enrich our prayer, they help us in our pilgrimage
through time and space; but in heaven a very different celebration

is taking place among the angels and saints! Even so, God is but one, and one too is Christ the Lord, who like a bridge joins earth to heaven. At this moment we feel closer than ever, sharing as it were in the liturgy of heaven.

"Blessed are those who have not seen and yet have come to believe" (Jn 20:29). In today's Gospel Jesus proclaims this beatitude: the beatitude of faith. For us, it is particularly striking because we are gathered to celebrate a beatification, but even more so because today the one proclaimed blessed is a Pope, a Successor of Peter, one who was called to confirm his brethren in the faith. John Paul II is blessed because of his faith, a strong, generous, and apostolic faith. We think at once of another beatitude: "Blessed are you, Simon, son of Jonah! For flesh and blood has not revealed this to you, but my Father in heaven" (Mt 16:17). What did our heavenly Father reveal to Simon? That Jesus is the Christ, the Son of the living God. Because of this faith, Simon becomes Peter, the rock on which Jesus can build his Church. The eternal beatitude of John Paul II, which today the Church rejoices to proclaim, is wholly contained in these sayings of Jesus: "Blessed are you, Simon" and "Blessed are those who have not seen and yet have come to believe!" It is the beatitude of faith, which John Paul II also received as a gift from God the Father for the building up of Christ's Church.

Our thoughts turn to yet another beatitude, one which appears in the Gospel before all others. It is the beatitude of the Virgin Mary, the Mother of the Redeemer. Mary, who had just conceived Jesus, was told by Saint Elizabeth: "Blessed is she who believed that there would be a fulfillment of what was spoken to her by the Lord" (Lk 1:45). The beatitude of faith has its model in Mary, and all of us rejoice that the beatification of John Paul II takes place on this first day of the month of Mary, beneath the maternal gaze of the one who by her faith sustained the faith of the Apostles and constantly sustains the faith of their successors, especially those called to occupy the Chair of Peter. Mary does not appear in the accounts of Christ's resurrection, yet hers is, as it were, a continual, hidden presence: she is the Mother to whom Jesus entrusted each of his disciples and the entire community. In particular we can see how Saint John and Saint Luke record the powerful, maternal presence of Mary in the passages preceding those read in today's Gospel and first reading. In the account of Jesus' death, Mary appears at the foot of the cross (Jn 19:25), and at the beginning of the Acts of the Apostles she is seen in the midst of the disciples gathered in prayer in the Upper Room (Acts 1:14).

Today's second reading also speaks to us of faith. Saint Peter himself, filled with spiritual enthusiasm, points out to the newly baptized the reason for their hope and their joy. I like to think how in this passage, at the beginning of his First Letter, Peter does not use language of exhortation; instead, he states a fact. He writes: "you *rejoice*", and he adds: "you *love* him; and even though you do not see him now, you *believe* in him and *rejoice* with an indescribable and glorious joy, for you *are receiving* the outcome of your faith, the salvation of your souls" (1 Pet 1:6, 8–9). All these verbs are in the indicative, because a new reality has come about in Christ's resurrection, a reality to which faith opens the door. "This is the Lord's doing", says the Psalm (118:23), and "it is marvelous in our eyes", the eyes of faith.

Dear brothers and sisters, today our eyes behold, in the full spiritual light of the risen Christ, the beloved and revered figure of John Paul II. Today his name is added to the host of those whom he proclaimed saints and blesseds during the almost twenty-seven years of his pontificate, thereby forcefully emphasizing the universal vocation to the heights of the Christian life, to holiness, taught by the conciliar Constitution on the Church, *Lumen Gentium*. All of us, as members of the people of God—bishops, priests, deacons, laity, men and women religious—are making our pilgrim way to the heavenly homeland where the Virgin Mary has preceded us, associated as she was in a unique and perfect way to the mystery of Christ and the Church. Karol Wojtyła took part in the Second Vatican Council, first as an auxiliary Bishop and then as Archbishop of Kraków. He was fully aware that the Council's decision to devote the last chapter of its Constitution on the Church to Mary meant that the Mother of the Redeemer is held up as an image and model of holiness for every Christian and for the entire Church. This was the theological vision which Blessed John Paul II discovered as a young man and subsequently maintained and deepened throughout his life. A vision which is expressed in the scriptural image of the crucified Christ with Mary, his Mother, at his side. This icon from the Gospel of John (19:25–27) was taken up in the episcopal and later the papal coat-of-arms of Karol Wojtyła: a golden cross with the letter "M" on the lower right and the motto *"Totus tuus"*, drawn from the well-known words of Saint Louis Marie Grignion de Montfort in which Karol Wojtyła found a guiding light for his life: *"Totus tuus ego sum et omnia mea tua sunt. Accipio te in mea omnia. Praebe mihi cor tuum, Maria*—I belong entirely to you, and all that I have is yours. I take you for my all. O Mary, give me your heart" (*Treatise on True Devotion to the Blessed Virgin*, 266).

In his Testament, the new Blessed wrote: "When, on 16 October 1978, the Conclave of Cardinals chose John Paul II, the Primate of Poland, Cardinal Stefan Wyszynski, said to me: 'The task of the new Pope will be to lead the Church into the Third Millennium.'" And the Pope added: "I would like once again to express my gratitude to the Holy Spirit for the great gift of the Second Vatican Council, to which, together with the whole Church—and especially with the whole episcopate—I feel indebted. I am convinced that it will long be granted to the new generations to draw from the treasures that this Council of the twentieth century has lavished upon us. As a bishop who took part in the Council from the first to the last day, I desire to entrust this great patrimony to all who are and will be called in the future to put it into practice. For my part, I thank the Eternal Shepherd, who has enabled me to serve this very great cause in the course of all the years of my Pontificate." And what is this "cause"? It is the same one that John Paul II presented during his first solemn Mass in Saint Peter's Square in the unforgettable words: "Do not be afraid! Open, open wide the doors to Christ!" What the newly elected Pope asked of everyone, he was himself the first to do: society, culture, political and economic systems he opened up to Christ, turning back with the strength of a titan—a strength which came to him from God—a tide which appeared irreversible. By his witness of faith, love, and apostolic courage, accompanied by great human charisma, this exemplary son of Poland helped believers throughout the world not to be afraid to be called Christian, to belong to the Church, to speak of the Gospel. In a word: he helped us not to fear the truth, because truth is the guarantee of liberty. To put it even more succinctly: he gave us the strength to believe in Christ, because Christ is *Redemptor hominis*, the Redeemer of man. This was the theme of his first encyclical and the thread which runs through all the others.

When Karol Wojtyła ascended to the throne of Peter, he brought with him a deep understanding of the difference between Marxism and Christianity, based on their respective visions of man. This was his message: man is the way of the Church, and Christ is the way of man. With this message, which is the great legacy of the Second Vatican Council and of its "helmsman", the Servant of God Pope Paul VI, John Paul II led the People of God across the threshold of the Third Millennium, which thanks to Christ he was able to call "the threshold of hope". Throughout the long journey of preparation for the great Jubilee he directed Christianity once again to the future, the future of God, which transcends history while nonetheless directly affecting it. He rightly reclaimed for Christianity that impulse of hope which had in some sense faltered before Marxism and the ideology of progress. He restored to Christianity its true face as a religion of hope, to be lived in history in an "Advent" spirit, in a personal and communitarian existence directed to Christ, the fullness of humanity and the fulfillment of all our longings for justice and peace.

Finally, on a more personal note, I would like to thank God for the gift of having worked for many years with Blessed Pope John Paul II. I had known him earlier and had esteemed him, but for twenty-three years, beginning in 1982 after he called me to Rome to be Prefect of the Congregation for the Doctrine of the Faith, I was at his side and came to revere him all the more. My own service was sustained by his spiritual depth and by the richness of his insights. His example of prayer continually impressed and edified me: he remained deeply united to God even amid the many demands of his ministry. Then too, there was his witness in suffering: the Lord gradually stripped him of everything, yet he remained ever a "rock", as Christ desired. His profound humility, grounded in close union with Christ, enabled him to continue to lead the Church and to give to the world a message which became all the more eloquent as his physical strength declined. In this way he lived out in an extraordinary way the vocation of every priest and bishop to become completely one with Jesus, whom he daily receives and offers in the Church.

Blessed are you, beloved Pope John Paul II, because you believed! Continue, we implore you, to sustain from heaven the faith of God's people. You often blessed us in this Square from the Apostolic Palace: Bless us, Holy Father! Amen.

IX

A Saint of Our Times

His Holiness Pope Francis I

HOMILY ON THE OCCASION OF THE CANONIZATION OF BLESSEDS JOHN XXIII AND JOHN PAUL II

Second Sunday of Easter (Divine Mercy Sunday), April 27, 2014

At the heart of this Sunday, which concludes the Octave of Easter and which Saint John Paul II wished to dedicate to Divine Mercy, are *the glorious wounds of the risen Jesus*.

He had already shown those wounds when he first appeared to the apostles on the very evening of that day following the Sabbath, the day of the Resurrection. But, as we have heard, *Thomas* was not there that evening, and when the others told him that they had seen the Lord, he replied that unless he himself saw and touched those wounds, he would not believe. A week later, Jesus appeared once more to the disciples gathered in the Upper Room. Thomas was also present; Jesus turned to him and told him to touch his wounds. Whereupon that man, so straightforward and accustomed to testing everything personally, knelt before Jesus with the words: "My Lord and my God!" (Jn 20:28).

The wounds of Jesus are *a scandal, a stumbling block for faith*, yet they are also *the test of faith*. That is why on the body of the risen Christ the wounds never pass away: they remain, for those wounds are the enduring sign of God's love for us. They are *essential for believing in God*. Not for believing that God exists, but for believing that *God is love, mercy, and faithfulness*. Saint Peter, quoting Isaiah, writes to Christians: "by his wounds you have been healed" (1 Pet 2:24, cf. Is 53:5).

Saint John XXIII and Saint John Paul II *were not afraid to look upon the wounds of Jesus, to touch his torn hands and his pierced side.* They were not ashamed of the flesh of Christ, they were not scandalized by him, by his cross; they did not despise the flesh of their brother (cf. Is 58:7), because they saw Jesus in every person who suffers and struggles.

These were two men of courage, filled with the *parrhesia* of the Holy Spirit, and they bore witness before the Church and the world to God's goodness and mercy.

They were priests and bishops and popes of the twentieth century. They lived through the tragic events of that century, but they were not overwhelmed by them. For them, God was more powerful; faith was more powerful—faith in Jesus Christ the Redeemer of man and the Lord of history; the mercy of God, shown by those five wounds, was more powerful; and more powerful too was the closeness of Mary our Mother.

In these two men, who looked upon the wounds of Christ and bore witness to his mercy, there dwelt *a living hope* and an *indescribable and glorious joy* (1 Pet 1:3,8). The hope and the joy that the risen Christ bestows on his disciples, the hope and the joy that nothing and no one can take from them. The *hope and joy of Easter*, forged in the crucible of self-denial, self-emptying, utter identification with sinners, even to the point of disgust at the bitterness of that chalice. Such were the hope and the joy that these two holy popes had received as a gift from the risen Lord and that they in turn bestowed in abundance upon the People of God, meriting our eternal gratitude.

This hope and this joy were palpable in the *earliest community of believers*, in Jerusalem, as we have heard in the Acts of the Apostles (cf. 2:42-47). It was a community that *lived the heart of the Gospel*, love and mercy, in simplicity and fraternity.

This is also the image of the Church that the Second Vatican Council set before us. John XXIII and John Paul II cooperated with the Holy Spirit in *renewing and updating the Church in keeping with her pristine features*, those features which the saints have given her throughout the centuries. Let us not forget that it is the saints who give direction and growth to the Church. In convening the Council, Saint John XXIII showed an exquisite *openness to the Holy Spirit*. He let himself be led, and he was for the Church a pastor, a servant-leader, guided by the Holy Spirit. This was his great service to the Church; for this reason I like to think of him as the *the pope of openness to the Holy Spirit*.

In his own service to the People of God, Saint John Paul II was *the pope of the family*. He himself once said that he wanted to be remembered as the pope of the family. I am particularly happy to point this out as we are in the process of *journeying with families toward the Synod on the family*. It is surely a journey that, from his place in heaven, he guides and sustains.

May these two new saints and shepherds of God's people intercede for the Church, so that during this two-year journey toward the Synod she may be open to the Holy Spirit in pastoral service to the family. May both of them teach us not to be scandalized by the wounds of Christ and to enter ever more deeply into the mystery of divine mercy, which always hopes and always forgives, because it always loves.

ACKNOWLEDGMENTS

The author thanks with profound emotion His Holiness, Pope Emeritus Benedict XVI, who in these pages also was willing to dedicate time, attention, and care to the memory of his saintly predecessor. And he wishes to express to all those who were interviewed his gratitude for their full cooperation and the sensitivity they showed, which made it possible to pay a tribute to Saint John Paul II that is unique and, at the same time, multicolored and polyphonic. Heartfelt thanks also to the editor for his attention and for the ideas he lavished in producing this book.

Finally, the author and the editor with one mind express their gratitude to *L'Osservatore romano*, to the news agency *Zenit*, and to the Polish weekly newspaper *Niedziela*, which over the course of recent years have published initial versions of some of the interviews, which were then revised and brought up to date, with the consent of those interviewed, for the present project.

NOTE ABOUT THE AUTHOR

Wlodzimierz Redzioch was born on September 1, 1951, in Często-chowa, Poland, and earned a degree from the school of engineering in that city. After continuing his studies at the University of Warsaw, at the Institute of African Studies, in 1980 he worked with the Center for Polish Pilgrims in Rome. During that period he prepared guide-books for Rome and the Holy Land in the Polish language. From 1981 to 2012, he worked for *L'Osservatore romano*. From 1995 he was a contributor to *Niedziela*, the most widely read Polish Catholic weekly newspaper, to *Inside the Vatican*, an American monthly maga-zine on Catholic topics, and to the news agency *Zenit*.

For his work as a Vaticanist, on September 23, 2000, he received in Poland the Catholic prize for journalism, "Mater Verbi"; in addition, on July 14, 2006, His Holiness Benedict XVI conferred on him the title of commander of the Order of Pope Saint Sylvester.

A prolific author, he has written various books about the Vatican (*La Tomba di San Pietro* [Calvarianum]; *In the Gardens of the Vati-can and Castel Gandolfo* [Sport i Turystyka]; *La Basilica di San Pietro* [Pallotinum II]; *Il Palazzo Apostolico* [Pallotynski Sekretariat Misyjny] and authoritative guides to the two principal Marian shrines (*Lourdes* [Pallotinum II], and *Fatima and Surroundings* [Plurigraf], both with an introduction by Cardinal Andrzej Maria Deskur). As the promoter in Poland of pilgrimages to Santiago de Compostela, he published *Santiago de Compostela: Il pellegrinaggio alla tomba di San Giacomo* (Pal-lotynski Sekretariat Misyjny) and the album *Il pellegrinare: Santiago de Compostela* (Bialy Kruk). Finally, he was co-author of a book on the day of prayer in Assisi: *Assisi: Incontro delle religioni del mondo* (Calva-rianum) and of an album by the photographer of the popes Grzegorz Galazka, *Cardinali del Terzo Millennio* (Libreria Editrice Vaticana).